Foreword

I am truly delighted to present to you the pages that await your exploration. The name **KK Vohra** carries a distinguished resonance among PEC alumni, renowned for their unwavering dedication and resilience. It is both an honor and a privilege for me to offer this foreword, not merely as a member of the esteemed Indian Administrative Service but also as a fellow alumnus of Punjab Engineering College, Chandigarh.

Though our respective journeys through PEC were separated by a decade, they share an unbreakable bond that is intricately woven into the very essence of our beloved institution. The corridors and lecture halls of PEC have borne witness to generations of passionate individuals who have passed through, each bearing the torch of innovation and the flame of progress. KK Vohra, an alumnus hailing from the Class of 1973, has carried this torch forward with an unwavering commitment.

In my interactions with KK Vohra, particularly during the events at PEC and the Alumni Association, I had the privilege of witnessing and supporting the extraordinary work that **KK Vohra** initiated as President of the Alumni Association. It was a period that marked a transformative chapter in the way our global PEC family connected and contributed. The first-ever Global Alumni Meet held in Houston, USA, during his tenure was a monumental effort to build bridges across PEC alumni worldwide.

It was heart-warming to witness **KK Vohra** channel his engineering acumen into innovative endeavors and foster connections within the PEC alumni community.

KK Vohra's remarkable journey, from his role as Engineer-in-Chief at the Punjab State Electricity Board to the insightful and inspiring narrative contained within these pages, epitomizes the spirit of lifelong learning and continual self-improvement. His experiences offer a wellspring of wisdom, a testament to resilience, and a guiding map for those in search of enduring happiness and fulfillment.

This book is a profound exploration of happiness and longevity, delving into the physical, mental, emotional, and spiritual facets of life. Drawing inspiration from the timeless wisdom of the Bhagavad Gita, it doesn't merely impart knowledge but equips us with practical tools to shape our lives.

As I reflect on my own journey, both in the civil services and as an alumnus of PEC, I am reminded of the common thread that binds our stories together—the unwavering belief that knowledge, dedication, and a sense of community can herald transformative change. In his book, KK Vohra encapsulates this belief, inviting you to embark on a journey of introspection and self-discovery.

Within these pages, you will uncover the profound truth that lasting happiness is not an abstract ideal but a tangible destination, and longevity is not a solitary quest but a journey interwoven with purpose. The book offers invaluable guidance for making the right life choices, recognizing the strength of spirituality in shaping our lives, and ultimately discovering joy, contentment, and purpose that extend well into a century and beyond.

Given KK Vohra's lifetime of dedication to both his profession and the pursuit of knowledge, I am confident that his insights and experiences will serve as a wellspring of inspiration for you.

It is my distinct pleasure to pen this foreword and introduce you to a book that is not just a collection of insights but a transformative journey.

I encourage you to embark on this journey with an open heart and a curious mind. As you turn the pages, may you unearth the profound secrets of lasting happiness and a roadmap for a life well lived.

DHARAM PAL, IAS
Adviser to the Administrator
U.T. Chandigarh

100 Years of Happiness

Authored by KK Vohra

CONTENTS

CHAPTER-1

Introduction

In the relentless march of our space age, humanity has achieved remarkable feats, from landing on the moon to venturing towards the possibility of life on Mars. The previous century bore witness to the birth of computers, televisions, mobile phones, missiles, and nuclear weapons—both tools of destruction and instruments of convenience. Today, our focus has shifted towards AI systems, drones, and even more potent weapons, amidst ominous talks of Star Wars. In the shadow of technological marvels, the realm of robotics has advanced so profoundly that we now contemplate companionship with humanoid robots. The field of medical science, too, has made incredible strides, producing life-saving drugs and techniques to extend our time on Earth.

Over the centuries, the concept of happiness and the parameters by which we define a fulfilling life have been in constant flux. One aspect, however, remains resolute amidst the changing tides of history: humanity's innate and unwavering desire to lead a long and happy life. Thankfully, with the rise in average life expectancy, crossing the threshold of a century of existence is no longer a utopian dream; it's a tangible reality. But within this potential lie two essential questions: Is longevity meaningful without happiness, and can we live to a hundred and beyond without experiencing the profound joys of life?

In a world that races ever forward, human desires have soared to new heights. The progress we've achieved, while promising comfort and convenience, often fails to alleviate the burdens of existence. Without a doubt, a successful career, a harmonious marriage, the home of our dreams and above all, good health are integral components of a fulfilled life. Yet the happiness we construct is often delicate and vulnerable to the vagaries of life. The pursuit of happiness is a complex endeavor. It's often elusive, akin to chasing a phantom. Despite the advances in science, there's no magic pill or fountain of youth to guarantee us a long, healthy, and happy life. However, happiness is also not a mirage, as is generally professed. True happiness requires an understanding of its dynamics, and this is where this book comes into play.

This book is an opportunity to delve deep into the reality of human existence and search for the secrets of happiness and longevity. Its goal is to provide a roadmap for laying a strong foundation for living and thriving into old age. It aims to set you on a path of action that will yield long-term benefits.

In the pages that follow, we explore the profound connections between mental well-being, emotional attitudes, physiological health, and enduring contentment. We come to realize that happiness is not a destination but a lifelong journey that demands consistent nurturing and sustenance. By delving into the intricate interplay of the physical, mental, emotional, and spiritual aspects of life, we uncover the keys to sustained happiness.

This book treats transformation as the cornerstone of a blissful life that extends beyond a century. It draws inspiration from the sacred wisdom of the Bhagavad Gita, a profound text that encapsulates India's Vedic wisdom and stands as one of the world's greatest spiritual and philosophical classics. We focus on the chapter "Bhagavad Gita: A Guide to a Fulfilled Life," delving into its teachings to navigate our worldly responsibilities selflessly, free from the shackles of material desires, while residing blissfully in this material realm. We will explore how the Bhagavad Gita's teachings provide profound insights and practical solutions, even in the face of life's most daunting challenges.

Throughout the chapters of this book, we examine the development of qualities essential for lasting happiness. You won't merely gain theoretical knowledge; you'll benefit from practical exercises, real-life examples, and step-by-step guidance on how to integrate these teachings into your daily life. Additionally, we discuss the significance of creating a blueprint for our lives—one that encompasses the subtle elements necessary for lasting happiness and longevity. Each chapter offers insights into different facets of nurturing enduring happiness, from physical vitality to mental well-being, and demonstrates how spiritual wisdom plays a pivotal role in achieving a fulfilling life.

The final chapter of this book provides a profound exploration of the experiences and realizations of the author during his formative years. From ambitious school days to transformative moments in his professional career, this chapter reflects on both his achievements and the opportunities that slipped through his grasp, underscoring the role of spirituality, resilience, self-belief, ambition, and the cultivation of meaningful relationships in shaping a life of contentment and purpose.

This book aims to guide you in realizing happiness within yourself and inspire you to spread happiness in the world. Its teachings hold valuable insights for adolescents and adults alike, illuminating the path to a fulfilling and joyful existence. Embarking on a journey of introspection and self-discovery, this book is an exploration of the author's life experiences, realizations and the profound impact of his beliefs on his path to lasting happiness.

This book is dedicated to two remarkable centenarians: Goodenough, the oldest Nobel Prize recipient at the age of 97, and Calyampudi Radhakrishna Rao, who received the International Prize in Statistics at the age of 102. Their lives serve as guiding stars for all who aspire to live a meaningful, fulfilled life beyond a century. We will delve into the commonalities that allowed these distinguished centenarians to thrive beyond 100 and also explore the lives of people residing in the six blue zones to uncover the shared factors that enable them to outlive us all. More than just a collection of insights, this book offers an interactive journey through the author's life experiences and realizations that led him to discover the secrets of lasting happiness. As you delve deeper into this exploration of happiness, you will open yourself to the possibility of a more meaningful and fulfilling existence. The path to lasting happiness may not be without its challenges, but by seizing control of your happiness with unwavering determination, the journey becomes more manageable. Within the pages of this book, you'll find valuable guidance for making the right life choices at the right times and understanding the strength of spirituality in shaping your life. You'll realize that lasting bliss and longevity are not distant dreams but transparent waters flowing steadily down the hills from a perennial spring.

Together, we will unlock the transformative potential of embracing our beliefs and experiences, leading us all to a life of enduring happiness. With practical tools, spiritual wisdom, and a supportive narrative, this book aims to guide you toward a life that brings joy, contentment, and purpose for a hundred years and beyond. Are you ready to embark on this journey within and discover the profound secrets of lasting happiness till 100? Let's begin together.

CHAPTER-2

100 Years of Happiness: Unveiling Secrets of Fulfillment

Have you ever contemplated living beyond 100? What does lasting happiness mean to you? Have you ever thought that blissful aging in the eighties and nineties needs strategic planning? Amidst the vast expanse of time and the human quest for a blissful existence, the elusive mirage of lasting happiness has captivated hearts and minds alike, inspiring countless journeys to unveil its secrets. Undoubtedly, a successful career, good health, and contentment are essential components of happiness. The world would become stagnant if humans lacked the ambition to excel in their endeavors to find happiness. Spreading happiness is itself a great source of blissfulness, which is recognized only by a few wise people. The world at large fails to overcome lust and greed, which are the causes of most of our miseries. We mistakenly associate happiness exclusively with the acquisition of power, position, wealth, and material possessions, only to find ourselves disenchanted once we obtain them. We fail to appreciate and savor what we already have, constantly yearning for more. Did you also ever find yourself chasing external markers of success only to feel unfulfilled once you achieved them? The world seems caught in a race to obtain everything that sparkles, yet even successful individuals can find themselves living in stress and depression. We begin by questioning the prevailing notion that equates happiness with external possessions, power, or societal status. While these external factors may bring temporary pleasure, they fall short of providing sustained happiness. Rather than material possessions, the true measure of happiness is whether you are at peace with yourself or not. And, are you having healthy biorhythms or not? True happiness originates from within, rooted in our perception, thoughts, and inner state of being.

You would appreciate that financial difficulties, relationship problems, and serious illnesses often disrupt our happiness. The reason may be our own mistakes or external factors beyond our reach. Paradoxically, some individuals live content lives with simple means, while others struggle despite the comforts of modern life. Happiness is more than fleeting positive emotions; it is a state of well-being that encompasses living a good life filled with meaning and deep contentment.

The renowned yoga guru and spiritual thinker, B.K.S. Iyengar, has very rightly said: In whatever position one is in, or in whatever condition in life one is placed, one must find balance. Balance is the state of the present—the here and now. If you balance in the present, you are living in eternity.[1]

While moments of joy bring temporary pleasure, lasting happiness involves navigating periods of discomfort and growth. Genetic makeup, life circumstances, achievements, relationships, and even neighbors influence our happiness levels. Stress arising from external challenges, our own attitudes, and negative emotions drains our energy. Think about a time when you faced adversity. How did you handle it, and what did you learn from the experience? Happy individuals possess emotional and mental resilience, experiencing the full range of emotions while maintaining an underlying sense of optimism. They have the ability to withstand adversity and

---

[1]B.K.S. Iyengar, John J. Evans, and Douglas Abrams (2006), "Light on Life: The Yoga Journey to Wholeness, Inner Peace, and Ultimate Freedom," p. 43, Rodale.

bounce back from difficult times in life. Do you agree that bouncing back in adversity lessens unhappiness and is the right approach to facing the challenges?

You need to understand that happiness is an ongoing pursuit that requires nurturing and sustenance. True fulfillment arises from contentment, meaningful connections, personal growth, and aligning our decisions with core values.

You would agree that health and happiness are intertwined, with physical well-being and self-care playing a vital role. Since the ages, it has been an innate desire of man to live a long life, happily. Thanks to advancements in medical research, the average life of humans has seen a significant rise. However, to ensure that those extra years added to life in the eighties and nineties are blissful, one needs to nurture the physical, mental, emotional, and spiritual realms coherently right from the young adult days. You would agree that the foundation for healthy and blissful aging ought to be laid in the early years of life. To lead a healthy, long, and happy life, we ought to understand the essence of true happiness and its role in creating blissfulness in our lives. Don't you feel that true happiness itself promotes longevity?

Undoubtedly, the priorities of life—health, career, relationships, money, power, and contentment—change with time. Health and spiritual blissfulness universally emerge as the top priorities in the last decades of life, and they complement each other remarkably in the symphony of happiness during aging. What are the top priorities in your life right now, and how have they evolved over the years? Are they comprehensively oriented towards blissful aging beyond 100?

Ultimately, understanding happiness is a lifelong quest. It requires a willingness to question conventional notions, explore different perspectives, and reflect on our own experiences. As we delve deeper into the exploration of happiness, we open ourselves to the possibility of a more meaningful and fulfilling existence.

In the 21st century, the quality of happiness is influenced by success in career, physical fitness, mental health, and the attainment of spiritual blissfulness—the coherence of body, heart, mind, and soul. The dynamics of happiness are so intricately intertwined that even the most successful people fail to balance the scales of happiness. The coherence of the spiritual, physical, mental, and emotional realms is the essence of a happy, healthy, and long life. To achieve this coherence is an art of living in which spiritual wisdom plays a lead role in guiding our actions and thoughts. As a result, the spiritual, mental, physical, and emotional realms blossom remarkably, leading to sustained happiness. Consider your own life. How do these realms interact, and what role does spirituality play, if any?

You may have noticed that blissfully happy people find joy in simple pleasures, live with meaning and purpose, have a belief in them, practice gratitude, maintain physical health, and nurture positive relationships. They avoid negativity, continuously learn from their experiences, and practice mindfulness. By becoming attuned to their thoughts, emotions, and inner state, they develop the capacity to choose their responses and cultivate a more positive and harmonious inner landscape. Their actions align with principles of universal consciousness, leading to a state of equipoise and engagement with absorbing activities. Which of these happiness signs do you resonate with the most, and which ones would you like to develop further in your life?

Spiritual blissfulness brings coherence to the mind, body, heart, and soul, which enhances well-being, cognitive performance, and synchronization of the body's systems. Positive emotions foster resilience and kinder responses to stress. Happy individuals regulate their emotions, maintain loving relationships, and exhibit integrity in the face of life's demands. The coherence of the spiritual, physical, mental, and emotional realms is the essence of a blissful and long life. In the upcoming chapters, we will endeavor to catalyze the harmony of soul, mind, and body, crafting a model for sustained happiness. Our exploration will shed light on the development of spiritual resilience, the nurturing of physical well-being, and the fostering of mental and emotional wellness. We will also create a blueprint for life with the goal of establishing a healthy and happy foundation to live and thrive into old age, with a particular focus on realizing the dream of blissfully aging beyond 100.

COHERENCE OF SPIRITUAL, PHYSICAL, EMOTIONAL AND MENTAL REALMS

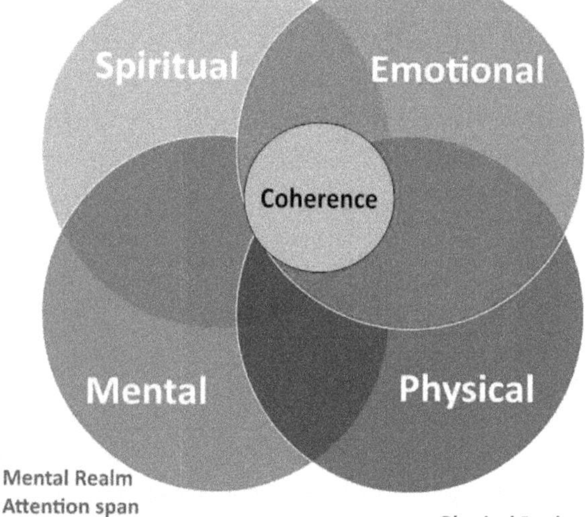

Yoga guru and spiritual thinker B.K.S. Iyengar says: When your body, mind, and soul are healthy and harmonious, you will bring health and harmony to the world—not by withdrawing from the world, but by being a healthy, living organ of the body of humanity.[2]

How do you interpret the connection between personal well-being and making a positive impact on the world?

In the next chapter, we will draw upon spiritual wisdom and timeless teachings to further illuminate the path to sustained happiness. We will uncover invaluable insights from ancient philosophies, sacred texts, and the wisdom of sages who have contemplated the nature of happiness throughout the ages. As we delve deeper into ancient philosophies and wisdom in the next chapter, think about how these timeless teachings might relate to your quest for happiness. What are you looking forward to discovering? Join us on this journey of self-discovery as we strive to unveil the essence of happiness and chart a course toward a more joyful and fulfilling life.

---

[2]B.KS. Iyengar, https://www.azquotes.com/quote/849981.

CHAPTER-3

Spiritual Wisdom: Our Actions, Thoughts, and Happiness

How do you relate our actions and thoughts to happiness? Have you ever consciously tried to improve your thoughts and actions? And if so, what was the result of your efforts?

In the previous chapter, we came to the profound realization that the coherence of the spiritual, mental, physical, and emotional domains is the essence of blissfulness. True happiness and lasting contentment cannot be found solely in the external world. While material possessions and worldly achievements may provide temporary pleasure, they do not guarantee sustained happiness. Insatiate desires or neglecting our health and relationships in the pursuit of achievements can all fracture the fragile happiness we construct.

The root cause of most of our miseries is sensual desires, which breed lust, greed, and attachment, and if the desires remain unfulfilled, they give rise to anger, disappointment, mental stress, and miseries. Lust for material objects deludes one's intellect, leading to unethical conduct, omissions, and the commission of negligence in the performance of one's multifarious duties. You may have noticed people committing blunders on account of their lust for sensual pleasures, money, or power. The temptations for sensual pleasures are too fierce to be controlled with a fickle mind. To transcend the bounds of misery and unhappiness, we need to venture into the realm of spiritual wisdom.

In a world often defined by chaos and uncertainty, spiritual wisdom becomes the compass that directs us toward the harbor of peace and contentment. It is sacred knowledge that empowers us to transcend the limitations of the material world and discover the eternal wellspring of joy that resides within us. As we walk this path of self-awareness and spiritual growth, we find that misery and unhappiness are but fleeting illusions, and true bliss lies in the embrace of our spirit. Spiritual wisdom helps you accomplish self-realization and guides you to perform your worldly duties righteously. It creates a space for self-improvement and encourages you to practice self-regulation and realize the presence of God at the center of the universe. By thinking from a higher level of conscience, we gain mental harmony, success in a career, and relationships. The goal of spirituality is to bring you happiness that nobody can take away from you.

Emphasizing the role of spiritual wisdom in creating lasting happiness, the renowned political philosopher, spiritual thinker, and father of the nation of India, Mahatma Gandhi, once said: Far more indispensable than food for the physical body is spiritual nourishment for the soul. One can do without food for a considerable time, but a man of the spirit cannot exist for a single second without spiritual nourishment.[3]

Let us understand how spiritual wisdom encourages righteous actions and thoughts.

1. Spiritual Wisdom for Righteous Actions and Thoughts:

Righteousness is an ideal path of life. All spiritual beliefs propagate righteous actions and thoughts. However, in the

---

[3]Mahatma Gandhi, Jawaharlal Nehru and Rabindranath Tagore (1968), "Wit and Wisdom of Gandhi, Nehru, and Tagore: Being a Treasury of Over Ten Thousand Invaluable and Inspiring Thoughts, Views, and Observations on About Eight Hundred Subjects of Popular Interest, Collected from the Speeches and Writings of These Three Great Leaders of Modern India."

absence of spiritual wisdom, righteousness becomes subjective, and one is often caught between the dilemmas of right and wrong. Spiritual wisdom refers to well-founded standards of right and wrong that prescribe what humans ought to do, usually in terms of rights, obligations, benefits to society, or fairness.

Spiritual wisdom helps us realize the presence of an Almighty God at the center of the universe. It teaches us about the existence of the soul in all living beings and the universal principles by which the universe operates. The spiritual energy that we draw from our faith in God and commitment to the principles of universal consciousness guides us to tread the path of life righteously. By thinking from a higher level of conscience, we nurture commitment to our deeper core values.

Contrary to misconceptions, spiritual wisdom does not encourage renunciation or retreating to the forests. Rather, it guides us to perform righteous actions aligned with our deeper values. The Bhagavad Gita, the essence of India's Vedic wisdom and a revered spiritual and philosophical classic, relates one's fortunes and misfortunes to the fruits of one's actions of the past and present births. The sacred book gives great importance to the performance of righteous actions, so much so that it describes the performance of worldly duties righteously without a feeling of sense desires as the easiest way of attaining salvation.

Mahatma Gandhi, the Father of the Nation of India, is an iconic figure known for his pursuit of spiritual wisdom and his unwavering commitment to non-violence and righteousness. Gandhi's life is a testament to how spiritual principles can guide one's actions and bring about profound change.

Gandhi's spiritual journey began with his experiences in South Africa, where he faced racial discrimination. He started to develop a deep sense of empathy and compassion for the oppressed. He adopted the principle of non-violent resistance (Satyagraha), inspired by the Bhagavad Gita and the teachings of Jesus Christ. Through acts of civil disobedience, fasting, and peaceful protests, he led India to independence from British rule. His spiritual wisdom not only played a pivotal role in India's freedom struggle but also continues to inspire movements for justice and civil rights worldwide.

Emphasizing the importance of righteousness in all walks of life, the Father of the Nation of India very rightly said: The main purpose of life is to live rightly, think rightly, and act rightly. The soul must languish when we give all our thoughts to the body.[4]

Dr. APJ Abdul Kalam, former President of India, popularly known as the Missile Man of India, was a highly spiritual man and an embodiment of righteousness. APJ Kalam, who was born into a poor rural family in Tamil Nadu, India, used to sell newspapers during school days to support his studies. However, he was spiritually inclined right from his childhood. In his book, Transcendence: My Experiences with Swami Pramukh Swami ji, he highlights the influence of spirituality on his mind from childhood and attributes his rise to the position of the President of India to God. Notwithstanding that he was a great scientist, he completely surrendered to God and advocated for the spiritual harmony of all religions. Emphasizing the role of righteousness at all levels, he once said: Where there is righteousness in the heart, there is beauty in the character. When there is beauty in the character, there is harmony in the

---

[4]Mahatma Gandhi, Anand T. Hingorani, Ganga Anand Hingorani (1985), The Encyclopedia of Gandhian Thoughts

home. When there is harmony in the home, there is order in the nation. When there is order in the nation, there is peace in the world. https://fb.watch/nylzfm6o7K/

The message by Dr. APJ Kalam is of far-reaching importance as it emphasizes righteousness as a tool for global peace. The mindset of the leaders is reflected in the policies of their governments. If individuals adopt the path of righteousness, they will elect leaders who believe in righteousness. If the people believe in righteousness based on principles of universal consciousness, there would be no issues of conflict among the countries, and the world would be a much more peaceful place.

2. Connection between Soul, Mind, and Body:

As a result of the deep link between mental and emotional attitudes, physiological health, and long-term well-being, our happiness revolves around our mind. That is why various spiritual beliefs preach us to elevate ourselves through the power of the mind and not to degrade ourselves, as the mind can be our friend and also an enemy. You ought to realize that power of mind if you aspire to achieve success in your career and relationships and lead a healthy and blissful life. Sense desires are like wildfires. They incessantly try to engulf the mind in their vicious circle of lust, greed, attachment, and anger, resulting in misery. Spiritual wisdom acts as a programming tool for the human mind, enabling positive thoughts and righteous actions, leading to sustained blissfulness. You might have noticed within you the ongoing battles between positive and negative tendencies, your higher aspirations and lower indulgences, and the conscious and subconscious mind. Amidst these ongoing battles, we ought to understand the dynamics of happiness in terms of the major forces at play within us: body, soul, mind, and heart. The thoughts that initiate human actions originate in the mind. They are guided by stimuli from the senses on the one hand and the soul on the other. The stimuli from the senses to the mind relate to pleasures, which are associated with vices like lust, anger, greed, and attachment. These vices form a powerful, vicious circle that incessantly tempts and traps the mind, eroding its intellect. Only the awakened soul, part of the divine power within us, can rein in sensual desires and shield the mind from their harmful grasp. Spiritual resilience manifests through a commitment to moral values, kindness, gratitude, love, and tolerance for others' beliefs. Do you ever face a situation where you are caught between the dilemma of deep core values and the temptations of sensual pleasures? The right approach in such situations is to listen to the voice of the soul. Every time you listen to your conscience, you build your spiritual resilience.

CONNECTION BETWEEN SOUL MIND AND BODY

SOUL
MORAL VALUES
GRATITUDE
TOLERANCE

MIND

THE BRAIN CONVERTS THE THOUGHT INTO SIGNALS TO OPERATE THE BODY

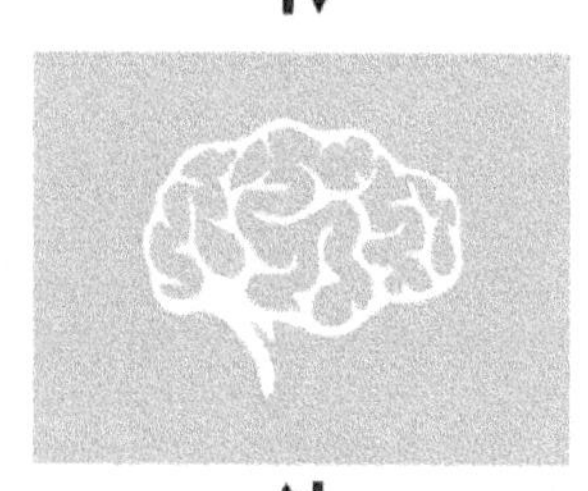

BODY
HEART
FIVE SENSES
- Hearing
- Sight
- Smell
- Taste
- Tough

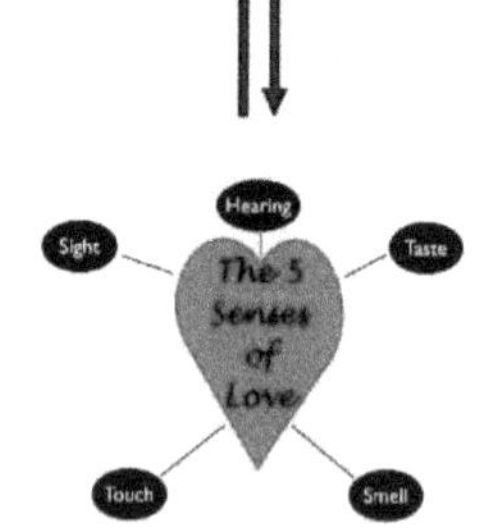

3. Spiritual Wisdom Creates Mental Harmony:

In the whirlwind of daily life, we often find ourselves entangled in desires, attachments, and fears that sow the seeds of misery and discontent. Spiritual wisdom offers us the transformative tools to break free from these self-imposed shackles. It invites us to practice detachment, letting go of the need to control outcomes, and finding peace in surrendering to the flow of life.

At its core, spiritual wisdom teaches us that happiness is an inside job. It is not contingent on external circumstances but springs from the depths of our consciousness. By cultivating a deeper understanding of ourselves and our connection to the world around us, we gain the ability to navigate life's ups and downs with equanimity.

Spiritual wisdom offers profound insights into the nature of existence, helping us understand the transient and impermanent nature of worldly pursuits. In the face of life's challenges and adversities, spiritual wisdom becomes our anchor, providing us solace and strength.

Through practices like meditation, self-reflection, and mindfulness, we can quiet the constant chatter of the mind and tap into a profound sense of inner tranquility. Spiritual wisdom teaches us that by observing our thoughts and emotions without judgment, we can detach from their fleeting nature and cultivate a sense of inner stillness.

Have you ever tried to observe your thoughts and emotions with the intention of improving them? If so, did you find any positive changes in yourself or your happiness level after that?

Spiritual wisdom helps us develop emotional regulation and practice self-regulation, cultivating gratitude, compassion, forgiveness, and control over lust, greed, and anger. Through forgiveness, we release the burden of past hurts and resentments, paving the way for healing and renewal. And by embracing gratitude, we shift our focus from what is lacking to what is abundant in our lives, thereby inviting more blessings to flow in. As we extend compassion to ourselves and others, we dissolve the barriers that separate us from one another, fostering a sense of interconnectedness and unity.

By overcoming our lust, greed, and anger, we alleviate our miseries and stress and nurture relationships, paving the way for mental harmony, success, and happiness in life.

The Yoga Sutra of Patanjali says, "When you are inspired by some great purpose, some extraordinary project, and all your thoughts break their bonds, your mind transcends limitations, your consciousness expands in every direction, and you find yourself in a new, great, and wonderful world, dormant forces, faculties, and talents become alive, and you discover yourself to be a greater person by far than you ever dreamed yourself to be."

Mother Teresa, a Catholic nun, exemplified the idea that true happiness is found in selfless service to others. Her life was a testament to the power of compassion, love, and spiritual wisdom.

Mother Teresa, originally from Macedonia, felt a calling to serve the poorest of the poor in the slums of Calcutta, India. She founded the Missionaries of Charity, an organization dedicated to helping the destitute, the sick, and the dying. Despite facing enormous challenges and often working in difficult conditions, Mother Teresa and her volunteers provided care and comfort to those in need. Her deep spirituality and unwavering dedication to serving others were a source of inner peace and contentment for her. She once said, "I have found the paradox that if you love until it hurts, there can be no more hurt, only more love." Her life of selfless service and spiritual wisdom continue to inspire people to find happiness in acts of kindness and compassion.

Mahatma Gandhi, Mother Teresa, and APJ Kalam were a few of the most outstanding personalities of this generation who integrated spiritual wisdom into their lives, guiding their actions and bringing about positive change in the world. They serve as powerful examples of how inner wisdom can lead to a life filled with purpose, happiness, and the betterment of society.

4. Spiritual Wisdom for Resilience:

Faith in a higher purpose, an essential component of spiritual wisdom, is a great source of strength. It grants us the courage to face difficulties with resilience and the faith that there is a higher purpose to our struggles. In times of adversity, spiritual wisdom becomes a lighthouse that guides us through the storm. It reminds us of the impermanence of challenges and instills in us the belief that even the darkest night will eventually give way to dawn.

5. Emotional Regulation:

Ultimately, the pursuit of spiritual wisdom is a journey of self-discovery and self-realization. It is an exploration of the vast inner landscape of our consciousness, where we unearth the profound truths that lead to lasting happiness. By embracing spiritual wisdom, we transcend the limitations of the ego and embrace the boundless expansiveness of our soul. For instance, consider how the practice of forgiveness, an aspect of many spiritual teachings, helps individuals release the burden of past hurts and resentments. This not only paves the way for healing but also fosters emotional well-being, allowing for a happier and more contented life.

Emphasizing the role of spiritual wisdom in creating lasting happiness, the renowned spiritual thinker Gurudev Sri Sri Ravi Shankar once said: I tell you, deep inside you is a fountain of bliss, a fountain of joy. Deep inside your center core are truth, light, and love; there is no guilt there, and there is no fear there. Psychologists have never looked deep enough.[5]

Let me share my personal experience of the happiness that spiritual wisdom brings. When one believes that this universe is a supernatural creation of God, who is omnipotent, omnipresent, and supreme, one's soul is awakened. An awakened soul recognizes God as kind and loving. Unflinching faith in God is a great strength. A spiritually inclined person is mindful of one's actions and thoughts; he believes in introspection and learns from his experiences, which make him navigate the journey of life joyfully. You might have also realized that the cause of most of our miseries is our failure to control our senses, which breed lust, greed, and anger. Undoubtedly, sensual desires are like wild horses and difficult to control. However, by understanding the miseries they create in our lives, we may, through practice, train our minds to control our senses. Introspection is a great tool of spiritual wisdom. By observing our thoughts and actions and challenging ourselves every time we feel like falling prey to sensual desires, we develop spiritual resilience. If we surrender to God and perform our worldly duties without a sense of desire, we attain

---

[5]Ravi Shankar, Ravi Shankar (Sri Sri) (2005), Wisdom for the New Millennium

happiness, which nobody can take away from us. We often take a great part of life to understand this truth of life. The earlier we realize it, the better it is.

6. Self-Regulation:

Spiritual wisdom empowers us to harness the power of our thoughts. We understand how optimistic thoughts can imbue us with a sense of harmony, fostering an uplifting atmosphere within our minds and hearts, while negative and self-defeating thoughts can plunge us into inner turmoil, leading to anxiety and distress. Spiritual wisdom guides us to become more mindful of our thought patterns. By learning to observe our thoughts non-judgmentally, we cultivate self-awareness and gain insights into the root causes of negativity.

The great spiritual thinker and philosopher Aristotle said: 'To know yourself, you must spend time with yourself; you must not be afraid to be alone. Knowing yourself is the beginning of all wisdom.'

Through various spiritual practices, such as meditation and introspection, we can develop the ability to redirect our thoughts toward positivity and purpose. This transformational process allows us to take charge of our mental landscape and foster a more resilient mindset. The most important relationship we can all have is the one we have with ourselves—the most important journey of self-discovery. As we delve deeper into the exploration of happiness, we open ourselves to the possibility of a more meaningful and fulfilling existence. Have you had any experience practicing meditation? Do you agree that making introspection a habit can bring positive changes in outlook, leading to sustained happiness and spiritual growth?

7. Spiritual Wisdom for Success in Career and Relationships:

Spiritual wisdom helps us realize our life's purpose and deeper values to effortlessly navigate the path of righteousness. The self-control imposed by the awakened soul fosters ideal human behavior and moral values, influencing our professional careers, marital lives, and other relationships. Our outlook towards life becomes positive, self-belief strengthens, and decision-making becomes more prompt. Spiritual energies create coherence among the physical, mental, emotional, and spiritual domains, leading to positive emotions, physiological efficiency, and self-regulation of the mind. Gratitude, love, and praise generate hormones that uplift our mood, while emotional regulation shields us from frustration, distress, and helplessness. This state of equipoise ensures smooth heart rhythms and breathing, improves immunity, and prevents serious health problems, enabling optimal functioning of our human machinery. The benefits include outstanding success in our careers, physical fitness, and a stress-free life filled with blissfulness.

Various spiritual beliefs emphasize faith in God, the presence of the soul, and actions inspired by universal consciousness. In this book, the spiritual beliefs draw inspiration from the philosophy of life based on actions (Karmas) as enshrined in the Bhagavad Gita. By following your own spiritual beliefs, you can also enlighten your souls.

In the next chapter, Bhagavad Gita: A Guide to a Fulfilled Life, we will immerse ourselves in the profound wisdom of this sacred text, delving deeper into its timeless teachings and uncovering the secrets to lasting happiness as illuminated by Lord Krishna. We would learn how spiritual wisdom helps you to accomplish self-realization, perform your worldly duties righteously, practice self-regulation, and realize the presence of God at the center of the universe, resulting in mental harmony and success in your career and relationships.

CHAPTER-4

Bhagavad Gita: A Guide to a Fulfilled Life

The Bhagavad Gita, the essence of India's Vedic wisdom, is a revered spiritual and philosophical classic and a model code of conduct for humankind. It encompasses teachings on the selfless performance of duties, the concept of humans as immortal souls, the administration of justice for human actions across lifetimes, and salvation as the ultimate goal of the soul. It has been revered for millennia as a timeless guide to living a meaningful and purposeful life.

The Bhagavad Gita is a sacred scripture of the Hindus, forming a part of the Indian epic, the Mahabharata. The Mahabharata is an ancient narrative that revolves around a great war between two factions of a royal family, the Kauravas and the Pandavas, who are cousins. In the midst of the battlefield of Kurukshetra, just before the commencement of the war, Arjuna, a warrior prince and a prominent member of the Pandavas, faces a moral dilemma. He becomes deeply troubled and conflicted about fighting against his own kin, teachers, and friends who are on the opposing side.

It is at this critical moment that Lord Krishna, the charioteer and divine guide of Arjuna, imparts his profound wisdom and teachings to help him overcome his inner turmoil. The conversation between Lord Krishna and Arjuna on the battlefield is the core essence of the Bhagavad Gita.

The Bhagavad Gita comprises 18 chapters, each addressing various aspects of life, duty, righteousness, spirituality, and the path to self-realization. It presents profound philosophical concepts and spiritual truths in a dialogue format, making it accessible to individuals from all walks of life.

The teachings of the Bhagavad Gita transcend time and culture, offering profound insights into human nature and the complexities of life. Throughout history, the Bhagavad Gita has influenced countless individuals and leaders across the world, inspiring them to seek higher truths, ethical values, and personal growth. The principles of the Bhagavad Gita continue to resonate with humanity as a whole, making it India's treasured gift to the world. The text's teachings have left an indelible mark on the fields of philosophy, psychology, ethics, and spirituality, and it remains a source of inspiration and guidance for seekers of wisdom and truth.

Annie Besant, an Irish socialist, theosophist, and women's rights activist, highlighted the significance of the Bhagavad Gita in her translated work titled The Lord's Song: "That the spiritual man need not be a recluse, that union with the divine life may be achieved and maintained in the midst of worldly affairs, that the obstacles to that union lie not outside us but within us—such is the central lesson of the Bhagavad Gita."

The teachings of the Bhagavad Gita highlight the root causes of human misery—lust, greed, attachment, and anger—which trap the mind in a vicious circle of desires. To overcome these tendencies, spiritual wisdom and self-control are essential. As explained earlier, the awakening of the soul acts as a protective shield, preventing the mind from succumbing to sensual desires. The Bhagavad Gita teaches us that by nurturing spiritual resilience through moral values such as kindness, gratitude, love, and tolerance, individuals can make righteous choices and maintain equilibrium even in challenging circumstances. By delving deep into the Bhagavad Gita and embracing its teachings, individuals can transform their actions and thoughts, fostering qualities such as decision-making ability, determination, truthfulness, tranquility of mind, thankfulness, compassion, performing duties selflessly, courage to fight injustice, love, kindness, righteousness, belief in oneself, clarity of mind, and a drive to achieve excellence.

Before we move forward to understand how various teachings of the sacred book can transform our lives into a blissful journey, let me explain that the sermon of the Bhagavad Gita was delivered by Lord Krishna to Arjuna when he was bewildered on the battlefield and refused out of fear and attachment to fight his kin and teacher. To bring Arjuna out of the dilemma and inspire him to fight for righteousness, Lord Krishna tells Arjuna, "All humans are immortal souls that take birth after birth till they attain the goal of attaining salvation. It's the mortal body that vanishes at the time of birth." Lord Krishna then urges Arjuna to shed feelings of attachment and fear and perform his sacred duty as a warrior: to fight. To reassure Arjuna of his duty, Lord Krishna dwells upon the Karma Philosophy of Life based on the fruits of the actions of the present and past births. Explaining to Arjuna the sacredness of one's duties, Lord Krishna says," The easiest way to attain salvation is the performance of worldly duties selflessly without any feeling of sensual desires." Lord Krishna then continues to preach to him the principles of universal consciousness and noble traits. He explains to Arjuna the relation between the soul and God, the path of meditation, the existence of God everywhere in all objects, and lastly, salvation, which is the ultimate goal of the soul. Lord Krishna displays sublime communication skills to bring home to Arjuna that the performance of his duties was most sacred and he would fall from grace if he failed to perform his duty.

By embracing the teachings of the Bhagavad Gita, we can transform our outlook and behavior, fostering qualities such as decision-making ability, determination, and truthfulness, tranquility of mind, compassion, and selfless dedication to our duties. This transformation empowers us to lead purposeful and meaningful lives, guided by the principles of righteousness and selflessness. Let us bask in the glory of the teachings of the Bhagavad Gita to lead a life of happiness, fulfillment, and purpose.

Section 1: Self Improvement for Happiness:

1: Performing Duties Selflessly:

We all know the importance of performing our duties. Whether to our family, workplace, society, nation, humankind, or our own selves, a sense of duty gives meaning and purpose to our existence. The Bhagavad Gita adds another dimension to the sacredness of duty by professing that duties should be performed without any sense of selfish interest or sensual desires.

Chapter 3 of the Bhagavad Gita introduces the concept of Karma Yoga, which describes the performance of righteous actions in the discharge of one's duties selflessly without any attachment to the fruits of the actions as the path to spiritual liberation.

Bhagavad Gita 3.19: [https://vivekavani.com/b3v19/]

Lord Krishna explains the importance of duty (dharma) and the performance of one's prescribed duties as per their position in society. He elaborates on how the world functions through the interplay of action and duty, highlighting that one should not avoid their responsibilities but instead fulfill them with dedication and integrity.

In Verse 30 of Chapter 3 of the Bhagavad Gita, urging Arjuna to perform his sacred duty to fight for righteousness without any desire or selfishness and with his mind free from mental grief, Lord Krishna preaches him to perform all works as an offering unto Him, constantly meditating on Him as the Supreme Lord.

Bhagavad Gita 3.30: [https://vivekavani.com/b3v30/]

As per Verses 4 to 7 of Chapter 3 of the Bhagavad Gita, one does not need to lead the life of a recluse to attain salvation, but instead, it guides us to perform righteous actions aligned with our deeper values.

Bhagavad Gita 3.4: [https://vivekavani.com/b3v4/]

Bhagavad Gita 3.5: [https://vivekavani.com/b3v5/]

Bhagavad Gita 3.6: [https://vivekavani.com/b3v6/]

Bhagavad Gita 3.7: [https://vivekavani.com/b3v7/]

Further verses 36 to 41 of Chapter 3 of the Bhagavad Gita preach us to perform actions without a feeling of sensual desires. The sacred book reminds us that the senses, mind, and intellect are said to be breeding grounds of desire; through them, it clouds one's knowledge and deludes the embodied soul. Lord Krishna emphasizes the necessity of overcoming selfish desires as well as ego-driven actions and tells Arjuna to conquer his senses and desires, as they are the root cause of attachment and suffering.

Bhagavad Gita 3.36: [https://vivekavani.com/b3v36/]

Bhagavad Gita 3.37: [https://vivekavani.com/b3v37/]

Bhagavad Gita 3.38: [https://vivekavani.com/b3v38/]

Bhagavad Gita 3.39: [https://vivekavani.com/b3v39/]

Bhagavad Gita 3.40: [https://vivekavani.com/b3v40/]

Bhagavad Gita 3.41: [https://vivekavani.com/b3v41/]

Verses 31 to 33 of Chapter 2 of the Bhagavad Gita guide us to perform actions righteously while discharging our duties. Lord Krishna reminds Arjuna of his sacred duty as a warrior and the righteousness of his actions as such, and he tells Arjuna that performing his duty as a warrior would bring him glory and a celestial abode, but if he abandons his duty to fight for righteousness, his image as a warrior would be tarnished.

Bhagavad Gita 2.31: [https://vivekavani.com/b2v31/]

Bhagavad Gita 2.32: [https://vivekavani.com/b2v32/]

Bhagavad Gita 2.33: [https://vivekavani.com/b2v33/]

The timeless teachings preach to us that actions driven by sensual desires are likely to bring misery. While performing our duties, we ought to keep in mind what actions we are supposed to perform as per the duties assigned to us, and furthermore, those actions should be performed without any selfishness or desires of the senses.

This principle applies to various aspects of contemporary life. For instance, a mother shouldn't let her attachment come in the way of her selfless performance of her duty of nurturing her children and instilling moral values. Leaders and administrators often face challenging decisions, and the Bhagavad Gita serves as a model code of conduct, guiding individuals in the performance of their duties without any consideration of power, lust, or greed.

In conclusion, by performing actions in the discharge of our duties selflessly without any feeling of desire, as per the teachings of the Bhagavad Gita, we rise above our interests and work for a higher cause. By following this timeless teaching, we contribute not only to personal growth but also to society. Not only this, but when all individuals undertake to perform their duties without selfishness and sensual desires, the world at large will be a much more harmonious place.

2: Ability to Take Prompt and Appropriate Decisions

In our lives, we constantly face important decisions, ranging from career choices to personal relationships. Making these decisions can leave us with negative emotions, disappointment, and regret if we lack self-reflection and fail to align our decisions with our major goals. It is crucial to connect decisions with our core values and avoid the trap of making choices solely based on comfort or social pressure. Also, decisions taken emotionally or with feelings of sensual desires are more than often bad decisions that may lead to misery and unhappiness.

Decision-making promptly and appropriately is even more critical in matters of national and international significance. Policy decisions driven by lust, greed, or attachment can have far-reaching consequences, potentially leading to disasters and chaos on a large scale. History is replete with examples where impulsive or self-serving decisions by leaders have caused immense suffering and upheaval. The wisdom of the Bhagavad Gita helps us develop the ability to take prompt and appropriate decisions that lay the foundation for sustained happiness.

The Bhagavad Gita emphasizes the importance of maintaining equipoise and cultivating mindfulness. The sacred book urges us to align our beliefs with deeper core values, enabling decisions based on intellect rather than emotions or sensual pleasures.

Verse 21 of Chapter 16 of the Bhagavad Gita warns that lust, anger, and greed are three gates leading to hell.

Bhagavad Gita 16.21: [https://vivekavani.com/b16v21/]

These vices obstruct our intellectual capacity and cloud our judgment. As discussed above, verses 36 to 41 of the Bhagavad Gita warn that sensual desires cloud one's knowledge and delude the embodied soul. To avoid unwise decisions leading to undesirable consequences, we ought to control our senses, as preached by the Bhagavad Gita.

The Bhagavad Gita reaffirms the significance of inner tranquility as a guiding force in our lives. The timeless wisdom reminds us that decisions made in deep anxiety or extreme elation can often prove to be sorrowful. In Verse 7 of Chapter 6, it is said that those who conquer their minds attain tranquility, and such individuals remain equipped in happiness or distress, heat or cold, and in honor or dishonor.

Bhagavad Gita 6.7: [https://vivekavani.com/b6v7/]

Imagine finding yourself in a highly elated mood due to some good news and then being tasked with making important decisions or passing orders. Under such circumstances, one's judgment may be clouded, leading to decisions lacking merit. Similarly, in times of distress, one may become too focused on one's sadness, hindering the ability to analyze matters effectively.

The American author, coach, and speaker, Tony Robbins, rightly said, "A decision made from fear is always the wrong decision."[6]

On the contrary, a tranquil mind forms the foundation for success, happiness, and growth. The Bhagavad Gita teaches us how to remain peaceful amidst the noise and confusion of the world. It advocates for a dynamic peace—a state in which the mind is at rest, the intellect sharp, and actions brilliant. Such peace is strong and resilient, not shattered by the changing and unpredictable nature of the world.

Furthermore, to make prompt and appropriate decisions, we ought to have faith and belief in ourselves and the higher power, which provides the needed strength and conviction. Verse 28 of Chapter 17 of the Bhagavad Gita reminds us that belief and faith are two strong pillars with which one can even move mountains, and any action that is done without faith is useless.

Bhagavad Gita: 17.28: [https://vivekavani.com/b17v28/]

By following the wisdom of the Bhagavad Gita, we develop the potential to cultivate equanimity and to make decisions based on our core values and intellect rather than those driven by fleeting emotions or sensual pleasures. The advantage of such an approach is not limited to individual well-being alone. It extends to the peace and harmony of the world at large. When leaders, policymakers, and individuals alike prioritize thoughtful and principled decision-making, the world can move towards a more stable and harmonious state.

---

[6]Tony Robbins Quotes: Fear, Decision, Made

In essence, the teachings of the Bhagavad Gita guide us toward the path of making decisions that are not only prompt and appropriate but also aligned with our deepest values and free from the sway of negative emotions. By embracing these teachings, we stand to gain not only sustained happiness as individuals but also contribute to global peace and harmony. In a world often characterized by chaos and impulsiveness, the Bhagavad Gita offers a timeless compass for decision-makers at all levels, reminding us that true wisdom lies in the pursuit of inner tranquility and the alignment of our actions with our core values rather than our emotions and selfish desires.

3: Maintaining Equipoise

In the vast tapestry of life, the Bhagavad Gita imparts a profound teaching to humanity—to maintain equipoise even in the face of the most challenging circumstances. Like a steady ship navigating turbulent waters, it urges us to train our minds to remain unaffected by moments of joy or sorrow. The sacred book preaches to us to maintain our composure even when provoked and to find a state of inner peace that remains unshaken by the ups and downs of life. By transcending the impulses of lust, anger, greed, and attachment, we find a profound sense of inner peace and resilience in the face of life's challenges.

Successfully treading the path of enlightenment requires high spirits and morale. One needs to overcome the negativities of the mind, such as sloth, ignorance, and attachment, and remain optimistic, enthusiastic, and energetic. Embracing success and failure, praise and criticism, pleasure and pain equally, is how we cultivate equanimity, as preached by the Bhagavad Gita. When we learn to navigate life's flux with tranquility, we gain a profound sense of inner fulfillment and lasting peace.

Seeing Arjuna overwhelmed with pity, his mind grief-stricken, and his eyes full of tears, in Verse 2 and 3 of Chapter 2 of the Bhagavad Gita, Lord Krishna tells Arjuna, "The delusion that has overcome you is not befitting an honorable person; it won't lead to the higher abodes, but instead to disgrace." Further, Lord Krishna urges Arjuna to give up petty weakness of heart and arise.

Bhagavad Gita 2.2: [https://vivekavani.com/b2v2/]

Bhagavad Gita 2.3: [https://vivekavani.com/b2v3/]

In Verse 48 of Chapter 2 of the Bhagavad Gita, Lord Krishna urges Arjuna to be steadfast in the performance of his duty, abandoning attachment to success and failure. Lord Krishna refers to such a state of mind as Yoga of Equanimity.

Bhagavad Gita 2.48: [https://vivekavani.com/b2v48/]

Emphasizing the importance of conquering the mind for attaining equipoise, Verse 7 of Chapter 6 of the Bhagavad Gita states, "Those persons who conquer their minds attain tranquility. Such individuals remain equipoise in happiness or distress, heat or cold, and in honor or dishonor."

Bhagavad Gita 6.7: [https://vivekavani.com/b6v7/]

Verse 20 of Chapter 5 of the Bhagavad Gita says: "A person who neither rejoices upon achieving something pleasant nor laments upon obtaining something unpleasant; who is self-intelligent; who is not bewildered; and who knows the science of God is already situated in transcendence."

Bhagavad Gita 5.20: [https://vivekavani.com/b5v20/]

The wisdom of the Bhagavad Gita is reflected in the words of Nobel Laureate and great spiritual thinker Dalai Lama: "With equanimity, you can deal with situations with calm and reason while keeping your inner happiness."

To attain such equipoise, persistent training of the mind and meditation are essential, as discussed later on in this chapter under the topic 'Meditation for Conquering the Mind: Dhayan Yog'. Achieving equipoise can be a game-changer for various professionals, including sportspersons, armed personnel, astronauts, politicians, administrators, lawyers, and actors. The teachings of the Bhagavad Gita offer a transformative approach to life—one that can lead to a profound shift in one's perspective and actions.

4. **Anger Management**

Anger is, undoubtedly, one of the major reasons for human suffering. When we let anger take control, we lose intellect and commit impulsive and regrettable actions that can be the cause of serious problems for us and others around us. The Bhagavad Gita warns about the destructive power of anger and its potential to cloud our judgment and reasoning. The sacred book proclaims that those under the control of anger possess a demonic nature, while those free from anger possess divine qualities. Lord Krishna declares anger to be one of the three gates to hell.

The Bhagavad Gita offers overcoming attachment to sense objects as a potent tool to overcome anger. Verses 62 and 63 of Chapter 2 of the Bhagavad Gita describe the relationship between lust and anger by stating that contemplation of sense objects breeds attachment for them, which further gives rise to desire for them, and from desire arises anger. It is further stated that anger gives rise to delusion, which leads to bewilderment, and bewilderment results in a complete loss of intellect. When intellect is lost, one is bound to be doomed. These verses highlight the dangerous chain reaction that anger can set off, leading us further away from sound judgment and rational thinking.

Bhagavad Gita 2.62: [https://vivekavani.com/b2v62/]

Verse 21 of Chapter 16 of the Bhagavad Gita categorizes lust, anger, and greed as the three gates leading to hell, emphasizing the need to overcome these negative emotions.

Bhagavad Gita 16.21: [https://vivekavani.com/b16v21/]

The wisdom of the Bhagavad Gita echoes in the words of Confucius, a great philosopher, teacher, and political theorist: "When anger rises, think of the consequences."

Verse 41 of Chapter 3 of the Bhagavad Gita urges that to develop control over anger, one should control one's senses to curb sinful lust, which is the destroyer of wisdom and knowledge.

Bhagavad Gita 3.41: [https://vivekavani.com/b3v41/]

When asked what impels individuals to sin, as if by force, even against their own will, Lord Krishna replies in verses 36 and 37 of the Bhagavad Gita that the root cause of the problem is lust, which, when unsatisfied, emerges as anger.

Bhagavad Gita 3.36: [https://vivekavani.com/b3v36/]

Bhagavad Gita 3.37: [https://vivekavani.com/b3v37/]

In Verse 39 of Chapter 3 of the Bhagavad Gita, lust has been described as a constant enemy of the wise because, like fire, it has an insatiable appetite. It cannot be satisfied for long. It envelops wisdom and gives rise to frustration and anger.

Bhagavad Gita 3.39: [https://vivekavani.com/b3v39/]

Lord Krishna time and again highlights the importance of equanimity of mind in life. Anger can never overpower the one who remains equipoise in success and failure, loss and gain, etc. Such a person focuses on the job at hand and is not worried about the results. He is not troubled by selfish desires, unreasonable expectations, or outbursts of anger.

In contemporary society, anger remains a significant challenge to our happiness. By training the mind through introspection and self-regulation, we can gradually gain control over the senses, which breed lust, the main cause of desires, and, in turn, anger. Equipoise, which acts as a shield from anger, may be developed through meditation and mindfulness. By following the teachings of the Bhagavad Gita, we may develop effective control over anger and avoid the unhappiness that often follows its unbridled expression.

5. Focus on Actions rather than Results: Overcoming Fear and Anxiety

Ironically, in this fast-progressing world, more people are coming into the grip of fear and anxiety. Anxiety sprouts from fear; it may be fear of failure in exams, career, competition, or relationship; or fear of losing money, a job, an election, or a match. The two negative emotions adversely impact peace and tranquility of mind, hampering the focus on the job at hand. Consequently, efficiency and the quality of work deteriorate. We often hear about students going into depression out of fear of unsatisfactory performance in exams or anxiety over their future. Obviously, due to anxiety and fear, incidents of suicide by well-established cinema and TV actors in India have registered a big rise in recent years. The Bhagavad Gita teaches us the importance of focusing on the present moment and the task at hand rather than worrying about the outcomes of our actions.

The Bhagavad Gita presents performing actions as a duty without attachment to the fruits of action as a tool to overcome anxiety and fear. As per Verse 19 of Chapter 3 of the Bhagavad Gita, performing actions as a duty without attachment to the results of actions leads to liberation from the cycle of death and rebirth.

Bhagavad Gita 3:19: [https://vivekavani.com/b3v19/]

By focusing on the actions rather than the results, we cultivate a state of complete tranquility, enabling actions without anxiety or fear. Verse 47 of Chapter 2 of the Bhagavad Gita says: You have the right to work only, and not to the fruits of work. Your motive should not be the fruit of your actions, nor should your attachment be to inaction.

Bhagavad Gita 2:47: [https://vivekavani.com/b2v47/]

Further, in Verse 48 of Chapter 2 of the Bhagavad Gita, Lord Krishna urges Arjuna to be steadfast in the performance of his duty, abandoning attachment to success and failure. Lord Krishna refers to such a state of mind as the Yoga of Equanimity.

Bhagavad Gita 2:48: [https://vivekavani.com/b2v48/]

Thus, the Bhagavad Gita preaches that while performing actions in discharge of our prescribed duties, our focus should be on the job at hand rather than the results of our actions. We are entitled to perform actions, but not to the fruits of those actions. Also, we are not supposed to abandon actions that we are supposed to perform as per the duties assigned to us because of fear of shame of failure, frustration of defeat, or disinterest in the actions. Fear and anxiety crop up when we start contemplating the results of our actions, and that leads to a loss of peace. If we put in our best efforts to perform the work in hand, keeping aside the outcomes, we can do our job with complete peace of mind, enhancing our focus on the work and efficiency.

This timeless teaching of the Bhagavad Gita illuminates our path at every step of life. Let us consider an example of a soldier fighting for his country. On the battlefield, he is not wary of the outcome of the battle and fights without any fear or bewilderment. He is bound to fail in the performance of his sacred duty as a soldier if, while fighting, he is overwhelmed by the considerations of his family. In Verse 51 of Chapter 2, Lord Krishna says that the wise, endowed with equanimity of intellect, abandon attachment to the fruits of actions, which bind one to the cycle of death and rebirth. By working in such a consciousness, they attain a state beyond all suffering.

Bhagavad Gita 2:51: [https://vivekavani.com/b2v51/]

By abandoning attachment to the outcomes of our actions, we free ourselves from unnecessary worries and anxieties, enabling us to perform our duties efficiently and effectively with a sense of purpose.

The wisdom of the Bhagavad Gita echoes in the words of the great basketball player Michael Jordan: "I would tell players to relax and never think about what's at stake. Just think about basketball. If you start to think about who is going to win the championship, you have lost your focus."[7]

---

[7]Michael Jordan AZ Quotes: Inspirational, Basketball, Winning

In today's fast-paced and outcome-driven world, individuals often become preoccupied with achieving specific results, leading to stress and disappointment when expectations are not met. By following the teachings of the Bhagavad Gita and dedicating our actions to a higher purpose, we can work with dedication and determination while remaining unperturbed by external circumstances.

Section 2: Bhagavad Gita for Righteous Living

1.   **Cultivating Virtuous Qualities**

The Bhagavad Gita encourages the cultivation of virtuous qualities such as fearlessness, truthfulness, determination, and compassion. By embracing these virtues, individuals can lead a life rooted in spiritual knowledge, nonviolence, modesty, and gentleness. Verses 1-3 of Chapter 16 of the Bhagavad Gita state that fearlessness, purity of mind, steadfastness in spiritual knowledge, charity, control of the senses, sacrifice, study of the sacred books, austerity, and straightforwardness; non-violence, truthfulness, absence of anger, renunciation, peacefulness, restraint from fault-finding, compassion toward all living beings, absence of covetousness, gentleness, modesty, and lack of fickleness; vigor, forgiveness, fortitude, cleanliness, bearing enmity toward none, and absence of vanity are the saintly virtues of the persons endowed with a divine nature. Such persons of divine nature are guided by the wisdom of the scriptures and uphold noble actions that bring positive effects to their minds and actions.

Bhagavad Gita 16:1: [https://vivekavani.com/b16v1/]

Verse 4 of Chapter 16 enumerates hypocrisy, arrogance, conceit, anger, harshness, and ignorance as the six qualities of those who possess a demonic nature.

Bhagavad Gita 16:4: [https://vivekavani.com/b16v4/]

In Verse 5 of Chapter 16 of the Bhagavad Gita, Lord Krishna inspires the cultivation of saintly qualities by saying that persons of divine nature get liberated from the bondage of cycles of birth, while those who possess demoniac qualities remain bonded to the cycle of births.

Bhagavad Gita 16:5: [https://vivekavani.com/b16v5/]

Further, Verse 24 of Chapter 16 of the Bhagavad Gita encourages guidance from the scriptures for understanding what should be done and what should not be done and performing actions accordingly.

Bhagavad Gita 16:24: [https://vivekavani.com/b16v24/]

Living at the level of our soul, we embody the essence of fearlessness and courage. By recognizing the imperishable nature of the soul, we are unshaken by doubts, insecurities, or fears. Cultivating these virtues can transform our behavior and success rate in life, allowing us to navigate challenges with grace and compassion and also helping us achieve our supreme goal.

2. Self-Control for Happiness

Self-control is one of the most important aspects of the teachings of the Bhagavad Gita. The text advises individuals to practice austerity and refrain from immoral and unethical practices. As per the Bhagavad Gita, sensual desires are the root cause of most of our miseries. Unbridled desires breed lust, greed, and anger, which in turn give rise to vices like untruthfulness, cheating, stealing, dishonesty, fault-finding, envy, immoral sex, wickedness, and other unethical practices.

When asked what impels individuals to sin, as if by force, even against their own will, Lord Krishna replies that the root cause of the problem is lust, which, when unsatisfied, emerges as anger. Verses 36 and 37 of Chapter 3 of the Bhagavad Gita describe lust as the all-devouring and most sinful enemy of mankind. In Verse 43 of Chapter 3 of the Bhagavad Gita, Lord Krishna says: Thus knowing the soul to be superior to the material intellect, O mighty-armed Arjuna, subdue the lower self (senses, mind, and intellect) by the higher self (strength of the soul), and kill this formidable enemy called lust.

Bhagavad Gita 3:43: [https://vivekavani.com/b3v43/]

The Vedic scriptures say that the biggest enemies—lust, anger, greed, envy, illusion, etc.—reside in our minds. The Bhagavad Gita offers elevating the mind as a tool for spiritual growth and happiness.

Verse 5 of Chapter 6 of the Bhagavad Gita says: Elevate yourself through the power of your mind, and not degrade yourself, for the mind can be the friend and also the enemy of the self.

Bhagavad Gita 6:5: [https://vivekavani.com/b6v5/]

Further, in Verse 6 of Chapter 6 of the Bhagavad Gita, it is stated that for those who have conquered the mind, it is their friend, and for those who have failed to do so, the mind works like an enemy.

Bhagavad Gita 6:6: [https://vivekavani.com/b6v6/]

The world-renowned spiritual leader Swami Vivekananda once observed in his speech delivered in San Francisco on April 5, 1900: "No two people see the same world. Some people who begin by saying that the world is a hell often end by saying that it is a heaven when they succeed in the practice of self-control.

If you can conserve and use the energy properly, it leads you to God. Inverted, it is hell itself."

The Bhagavad Gita suggests that we may purify our minds and overcome the lust responsible for our sins by listening to the voice of the soul. When we become receptive to the knowledge of the eternal essence, avoiding harmful behavior, our spiritual energies increase. And we perform only righteous actions.

Though a challenging task, exercising self-control is critical for personal growth and spiritual development. By raising our spiritual energies and by practicing, we may overcome the impulses of lust, greed, and anger that may otherwise lead us astray. We will learn about conquering mind in the succeeding pages of the chapter under the topic 'Meditation for Conquering Mind: Dhayan Yog.'

3.   Sattvik Actions, Food, Sacrifice, and Austerities:

The Bhagavad Gita encourages Sattvik actions guided by the spiritual wisdom of the scriptures rather than those driven solely by sensual desires. As per the sacred text, Sattvik actions, performed selflessly and dedicated to a higher purpose, bring clarity and fulfillment.

Verses 5 and 6 of Chapter 14 of the Bhagavad Gita say that Prakriti, or material nature, is made up of three Guṇas or modes—Sattva (goodness), Rajas (passion), and Tamas (ignorance). These modes bind the eternal soul to the perishable body. Amongst these, Sattva Guṇa, the mode of goodness, being purer than the others, is illuminating and full of well-being. It binds the soul by creating attachment for a sense of happiness and knowledge. Humans, food, sacrifice, and austerities of Sattva modes, or Gunas, are referred to as of Sattvik nature in the text.

Bhagavad Gita 14:5: [https://vivekavani.com/b14v5/]

Bhagavad Gita 14:6: [https://vivekavani.com/b14v6/]

Verse 16 of Chapter 14 of the Bhagavad Gita encourages us to perform Sattvik actions that are performed in the mode of goodness, as they bestow pure results. It further says that actions performed in the mode of passion result in pain, and those in the mode of ignorance result in darkness.

Bhagavad Gita 14:16: [https://vivekavani.com/b14v16/]

The Bhagavad Gita elaborates on the characteristics of Sattvik persons as truth, purity, peace, happiness, wisdom, harmony, and illumination in every aspect of life. With a steady mind, they make selfless decisions because that is the right thing to do. Clarity, creative and intuitive thinking, spiritual energy, and benevolence characterize Sattva Gunas. The sacred text advises against food, charity, and sacrifice that promote passion and ignorance. Instead, it urges us to reduce and eventually eliminate actions rooted in passion and ignorance, purifying our minds and preparing us to absorb spiritual knowledge.

Verse 14 of Chapter 17 of the Bhagavad Gita describes Sattvik austerities of words, body, and mind.

Bhagavad Gita 17:14: [https://vivekavani.com/b17v14/]

When devout people with ardent faith practice these three-fold austerities without yearning for material rewards, they are designated as austerities in the mode of goodness.

Bhagavad Gita 17:17: [https://vivekavani.com/b17v17/]

Verses 8, 11, and 20 of Chapter 17 of the Bhagavad Gita describe Sattvik food, sacrifice, and charity based on their benevolent nature and good effects on the life span, virtues, strength, health, mind, and happiness.

Bhagavad Gita 17:8: [https://vivekavani.com/b17v8/]

Bhagavad Gita 17:11: [https://vivekavani.com/b17v11/]

Bhagavad Gita 17:20: [https://vivekavani.com/b17v20/]

Success in a career and in relationships depends upon our actions and thoughts, which are strongly influenced by the state of our mind and physical health. By dedicating our actions, thoughts, and even food to God, we become more mindful of our choices and actions, leading ourselves toward righteous and ethical behavior. By leading a Sattvik life, as preached in the Bhagavad Gita, we cultivate spiritual growth and blissfulness.

4. Forgiveness and compassion

Forgiveness is promoted as a virtue in the Bhagavad Gita. By cultivating an attitude of forgiveness toward others, we release feelings of anger, resentment, and revenge. Forgiveness contributes to the development of a compassionate and peaceful mind. Forgiving others not only benefits the person being forgiven but also brings inner peace and emotional healing to the one who forgives. The Bhagavad describes forgiveness, compassion, and humility as the virtues of persons with a divine nature. Forgiveness and compassion belong to a state of higher mind.

In Verses 1 to 3 of Chapter 16 of the Bhagavad Gita, Lord Krishna enumerates fearlessness, purity of mind, steadfastness in spiritual knowledge, charity, control of the senses, sacrifice, study of the sacred books, austerity, straightforwardness, non-violence, truthfulness, absence of anger, renunciation, peacefulness, restraint from fault-finding, compassion towards all living beings, absence of covetousness, gentleness, modesty, and absence of fickleness; vigor, forgiveness, fortitude, cleanliness, absence of enmity, as virtues of those endowed with a divine nature.

Bhagavad Gita 16:1: [https://vivekavani.com/b16v1/]

Further, verses 8 to 12 of Chapter 13 of the Bhagavad Gita describe forgiveness, non-violence, steadfastness, self-control, nonattachment, and devotion to God as part of knowledge, and all that is contrary to that as ignorance.

Bhagavad Gita 13:8: [https://vivekavani.com/b13v8/]

The Bhagavad Gita describes compassion for all living beings as a great virtue of the devotees and describes all living beings—humans, animals, and plants—as members of the divine family. In Verse 32 of Chapter 6 of the Bhagavad Gita, Lord Krishna says: "I regard him as a perfect yogi who sees the true equality of all living beings and responds to the joys and sorrows of others as if they were his own."

Bhagavad Gita 6:32: [https://vivekavani.com/b6v32/]

Furthermore, in Verse 13 of Chapter 12 of the Bhagavad Gita, Lord Krishna says: "My true devotee does not feel hatred for any being but is friendly and compassionate towards all, without the thoughts of I and mine."

Bhagavad Gita 12.13: [https://vivekavani.com/b12v13/]

The Bhagavad Gita time and again lays great emphasis on treating all living beings equally, as illustrated in the topic of universal consciousness in the succeeding pages of this chapter.

In conclusion, forgiveness and compassion belong to a state of higher mind, which leads to inner peace, spiritual growth, and happiness. We may develop forgiveness and compassion through the purification of the mind, as illustrated under the topic 'Meditation for Conquering Mind: Dhayan Yog' in the succeeding pages of this chapter. Let us follow the teachings of the Bhagavad Gita to develop forgiveness and compassion and illuminate our lives with blissfulness.

Section 3: Bhagavad Gita for Spiritual Awakening

1. Universal Consciousness

The concept of universal consciousness is a profound and central theme in the Bhagavad Gita. It serves as the spiritual cornerstone that unites all living beings through the eternal truth of God, the souls that reside within their physical bodies, and the encompassing material nature. In the Bhagavad Gita, it is reiterated time and again that all living beings are, at their core, souls. These souls are eternal, as is the presence of God and the material world. God, often referred to as the Supreme Soul, exists within and beyond all living entities. He is the creator, preserver, and destroyer of the universe. The sacred text encourages us to adopt an all-encompassing perspective, viewing every living being with equal vision while recognizing the divine essence in each. This profound outlook fosters unity, compassion, and an overwhelming sense of oneness with the universe itself. Let us see what the teachings of the Bhagavad Gita say about the principles of universal consciousness:

Verse 31 of Chapter 13 of the Bhagavad Gita strongly advocates the principles of universal consciousness by saying that those who see the diverse variety of living beings situated in the same material nature and understand all of them to be born from it attain the realization of God (Brahman).

This interconnectedness underscores the essence of universal consciousness, emphasizing the unity that binds all life.

Bhagavad Gita 13:31: [https://vivekavani.com/b13v31/]

Verse 18 of Chapter 5 of the Bhagavad Gita underscores the importance of treating all living beings with equality and compassion. It declares that individuals who possess divine knowledge view every being, whether an upper-caste person (Brahmin), a cow, an elephant, a dog, or even a dog-eater, with the same vision. This equanimity in perception reflects the essence of universal consciousness.

Bhagavad Gita 5:18: [https://vivekavani.com/b5v18/]

Building on the theme of equality in vision, Verse 19 of Chapter 5 explains that those who establish their minds in the principles of equal vision conquer the cycle of birth and death. They embody the qualities of God and are seated in the Absolute Truth. Regardless of their present circumstances, they will attain liberation, reflecting the transformative power of universal consciousness.

Bhagavad Gita 5:19: [https://vivekavani.com/b5v19/]

In Verse 20 of Chapter 10, Lord Krishna reveals his omnipresence and connection to all living entities. He declares that He resides in the hearts of every living being, serving as the beginning, middle, and end of all existence. This emphasizes the idea that universal consciousness connects and sustains all life.

Bhagavad Gita 10:20: [https://vivekavani.com/b10v20/]

Verse 25 of Chapter 5 of the Bhagavad Gita encourages individuals to dedicate themselves to the well-being of all living beings. It states that those who have purged themselves of sin, eradicated doubt, disciplined their minds, and are devoted to the welfare of all creatures will attain God and be liberated from material existence.

Bhagavad Gita 5:25: [https://vivekavani.com/b5v25/]

In conclusion, the Bhagavad Gita unequivocally asserts that all living beings are creations of the Almighty God and should be treated with equality and compassion. Universal Consciousness emphasizes that the Supreme Soul resides within the essence of every living being, connecting them through a shared divine presence. Additionally, the text underscores the significance of dedicating oneself to the welfare of all beings on the path to spiritual enlightenment.

By acknowledging the interconnectedness of all life, we become more empathetic and compassionate toward others. When we recognize the divine presence in everything, we transcend feelings of separation and embrace a broader sense of belonging and love, cultivating happiness. Universal consciousness serves as a guiding light, illuminating the path to profound spiritual awakening and unity with the universe.

2. Faith in God: Nurturing Blissfulness

Have you ever tried to imagine the supernatural design of this universe with billions of solar systems like ours revolving around a black hole in the Milky Way galaxy and further billions of such galaxies with their own billions of solar systems revolving around their own black holes? Perhaps you have noticed that the basic structure of an atom with the electrons orbiting the neutron at the center of the earth is similar to that of our solar system, with the planets revolving around the sun at the center of the solar system.

And billions of such solar systems revolve around a black hole in their galaxies in a similar manner. Furthermore, billions of galaxies revolve, along with their solar systems, around another super black hole in a similar manner. There are countless unique species of animals and plants in this universe. The human body is itself a superstructure, with various organs working wonderfully in coordination. Isn't it a supernatural design of our universe? Looking at the supernatural design of this universe, a large section of scientists has also now started believing in the existence of God.

Faith in God is presented as a source of strength and guidance in the Bhagavad Gita. Trusting in a higher power provides hope, positivity, and purpose in life. By dedicating our actions to God and surrendering the results to His will, we discover solace and reassurance in our journey.

- **God is Supreme:** Faith in God means believing that He is Supreme, omnipresent, omnipotent, omniscient, and the creator of this universe. And our actions are subject to divine justice.

Verse 3 of Chapter 10 of the Bhagavad Gita says that God is unborn, without a beginning, and the Supreme Lord of the universe.

Bhagavad Gita 10:3: [https://vivekavani.com/b10v3/]

Verse 8 of Chapter 10 of the Bhagavad Gita says that God is the origin of all creation, and everything proceeds from Him.

Bhagavad Gita 10:8: [https://vivekavani.com/b10v8/]

Verse 18 of Chapter 9 says that God is the Preserver, Creator, and Destroyer of this universe and the supreme goal of all living beings. The verse further describes God as the Master, Witness, Abode, Shelter, Friend, the Origin and the End, and the Eternal Seed.

Bhagavad Gita 9:18: [https://vivekavani.com/b9v18/]

Verses 15 to 18 of Chapter 10 of the Bhagavad Gita describe God as a Supreme Personality with inconceivable energy, the Creator and Lord of all beings, the God of all gods, and the Lord of the universe.

Bhagavad Gita 10:15: [https://vivekavani.com/b10v15/]

Bhagavad Gita 10:16: [https://vivekavani.com/b10v16/]

Bhagavad Gita 10:17: [https://vivekavani.com/b10v17/]

Bhagavad Gita 10:18: [https://vivekavani.com/b10v18/]

- **Faith in God: Illuminating the Mind:** Those who have deep faith in God do not blame their fortune. God enlightens them with knowledge. They learn from the experiences of life and lead a life of contentment and fulfillment.

In Verses 10 and 11 of Chapter 10 of the Bhagavad Gita, Lord Krishna says that to those whose minds are always united with God in loving devotion, He gives them divine knowledge by which they can attain Him. Out of compassion for them, He dwells within their hearts and destroys the darkness born of ignorance with the luminous lamp of knowledge.

Bhagavad Gita 10:10: [https://vivekavani.com/b10v10/]

Bhagavad Gita 10:11: [https://vivekavani.com/b10v11/]

Recognizing God's presence at the core of the universe, we commit to performing righteous actions, nurturing compassion and kindness toward others, exercising self-control, and subjecting ourselves to self-reflection. The benefits of this practice are manifold and include self-improvement, success in career and relationships, improved physical and mental health, and ultimately, the path to blissfulness, accompanied by spiritual growth.

Verse 22 of Chapter 9 of the Bhagavad Gita assures that God is kind and loves His devotees, and those who maintain steadfastness in Him and righteousness are assured of victory. Further, He provides His devotees with all that they lack and preserves what they have.

Bhagavad Gita 9:22: [https://vivekavani.com/9v22/]

- **Faith in God: Inner Strength:** Faith in God imparts inner strength and provides a sense of purpose, particularly in trying times. Those with strong faith in God develop an inner resilience that allows them to rebound in the face of adversity and suffering.

Emphasizing the importance of faith in God, John C. Maxwell says, "Give God the first part of every day. Give God the first day of every week. Give God the first portion of your income. Give God the first consideration in every decision. Give God the first place in your life."[8]

By nurturing their faith in God, as advocated in the Bhagavad Gita, individuals develop compassion, positivity, self-control, and kindness, fostering a life filled with optimism and eventual

---

[8]John C. Maxwell (2007), "Leadership Principles for Graduates: Create Success in Life One Day at a Time," p. 114, Thomas Nelson Inc.

bliss. The Bhagavad Gita describes the ultimate goal of the soul as merging with God, or achieving Moksha. The text delineates three paths for the soul to unite with God: the Yoga of Knowledge (Gyan Yoga), the Yoga of Action (Karma Yoga), and the Yoga of Devotion, or Bhakti Yoga. Strengthening our faith in God, as expounded in the Bhagavad Gita, offers a roadmap to a fulfilling life brimming with compassion and positivity.

3. Meditation for Conquering the Mind: Dhayan Yog

The Bhagavad Gita presents meditation as a tool for purifying the mind. It is a path of self-realization and union with the divine. By practicing meditation, we may cultivate physical and mental discipline, leading to spiritual growth and inner peace. The Yoga of Meditation revealed by Lord Krishna is compiled in Chapter 6 of the Bhagavad Gita and referred to as Dhayan Yog.

Lord Krishna explains to Arjuna the yoga of meditation and methods of practicing it. He also talks about the role of action in preparing for meditation and how performing duties in devotion purifies one's mind and heightens one's spiritual consciousness.

Verses 13 to 14 of Chapter 6 of the Bhagavad Gita say: Seated firmly on a seat, in a sanctified place, made by placing grass, deerskin, and a cloth, one over the other, the yogi should strive to purify the mind by focusing it in meditation with one-pointed concentration, controlling all thoughts and activities. He must hold the body, neck, and head firmly in a straight line and gaze at the tip of the nose without allowing the eyes to wander.

Bhagavad Gita 6:13: [https://vivekavani.com/b6v13/]

Verse 15 of Chapter 6 of the Bhagavad Gita says that through meditation, one can quiet the restless mind, connect with the true self, and attain liberation from the cycle of rebirth.

Bhagavad Gita 6:15: [https://vivekavani.com/b6v15/]

In Chapter 6 of the Bhagavad Gita, Lord Krishna also explains the obstacles that one faces when trying to control one's mind and the working methods by which one can conquer one's mind. In Verses 35 and 36 of Chapter 6 of the Bhagavad Gita, Lord Krishna says that the mind is indeed very difficult to restrain, but with practice and detachment, it can be controlled. Lord Krishna also reveals how individuals can focus their minds on God and unite with Him.

Bhagavad Gita 6:35: [https://vivekavani.com/b6v35/]

Bhagavad Gita 6:36: [https://vivekavani.com/b6v36/]

Verses 24 to 25 of Chapter 6 of the Bhagavad Gita say: Completely renouncing all desires arising from thoughts of the world, one should restrain the senses from all sides with the mind. Slowly and steadily, with conviction in the intellect, the mind will become fixed on God alone and will think of nothing else.

Bhagavad Gita 6:24: [https://vivekavani.com/b6v24/]

Verse 28 of Chapter 6 of the Bhagavad Gita states: The self-controlled yogi, thus uniting the self with God, becomes free from material contamination, and being in constant touch with the Supreme Lord, achieves the highest state of perfect happiness.

Bhagavad Gita 6:28: [https://vivekavani.com/b6v28/]

Meditation is a path of self-realization and union with the divine. By practicing meditation, we may cultivate physical and mental discipline, leading to spiritual growth and inner peace. Meditation is a path of self-realization and union with the divine.

It helps us experience inner transformation, leading to a more profound understanding of ourselves and our place in the universe. By practicing meditation, we may cultivate physical and mental discipline, leading to spiritual growth and inner peace.

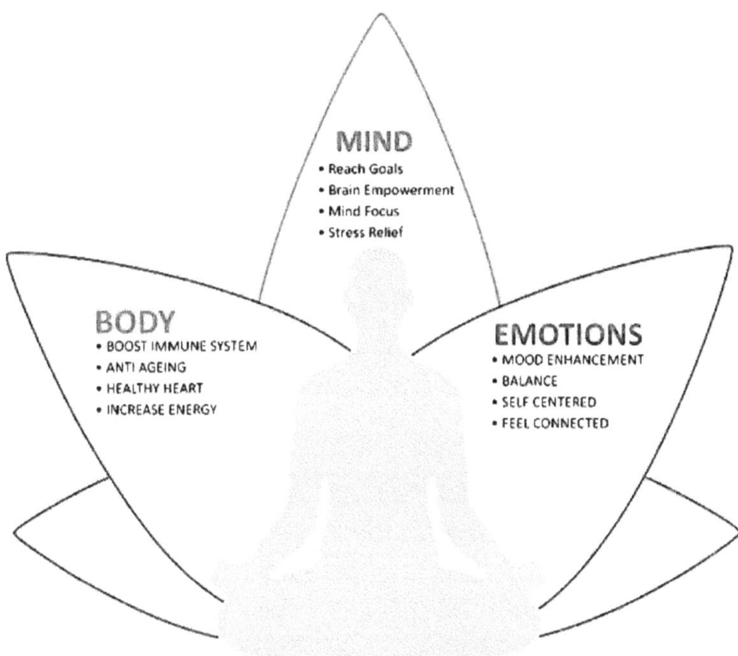

Benefits of Meditation

Section 4: Bhagavad Gita for Self-Regulation and Personal Growth

1. Self-Introspection for Fulfillment

Self-introspection, literally meaning to look within, stands as an essential pillar of personal growth and spiritual development. The Bhagavad Gita encourages individuals to delve into the depths of their thoughts, actions, and motivations with unwavering honesty. As we've gleaned from Chapter 2, the mind assumes a central role in sustaining happiness, influencing success in careers and relationships, nurturing mental and physical health, and fostering spiritual growth. In Bhagavad Gita's wisdom, the mind emerges as our ally when elevated and our adversary when degraded.

- **Significance of Introspection:** In our journey through this world, we find ourselves influenced by a myriad of external stimuli. Thanks to our senses, we form attachments and aversions to these stimuli, thereby giving birth to desires. Our actions are driven by sensual desires that lead to misery if our mind heeds them over the voice of our soul. However, the beauty of human existence lies in our capacity for self-correction, and self-introspection serves as the essential compass for this journey.

- **Self-Introspection for Improvement:** Self-introspection is a potent tool for improving our behavior, conduct, and efforts. It paves the path towards success in career, relationships, and better health. Yet its true value manifests when we consider its role as an enlightened soul. The spiritual enlightenment that guides our introspection is rooted in attaining wisdom from the sacred scriptures.

- **Guidance from the Scriptures**: Verse 24 of Chapter 16 of the Bhagavad Gita says: "Let the scriptures be your authority in determining what should be done and what should not be done. Understand the scriptural injunctions and teachings, and then perform your actions in this world accordingly."

Bhagavad Gita 16:24: [https://vivekavani.com/b16v24/]

Our spiritual resilience acts as a vigilant guardian, sounding the alarm when we deviate from our core values. In this eternal battle, self-introspection becomes our lifeline against sensual desires, which resemble an uncontrolled wildfire threatening to consume us with lust, greed, anger, and other vices that breed misery. By regularly reflecting on our behavior, we identify areas ripe for improvement, allowing us to recalibrate our lives according to righteous principles. Through this ongoing process of self-awareness and introspection, we adapt gracefully to new circumstances, ultimately nurturing a harmonious and balanced life.

2. Resilience and Inner Strength

Happiness is not the absence of difficulties in life but instead includes the capacity to bounce back from adversity, trauma, tragedy, threats, or stress. Resilience is the capability to hold out against crises and threats and regain stability quickly. We face difficult situations due to our own mistakes and external factors beyond our control, including natural calamities. The Bhagavad Gita is a classical philosophy of life offering solutions for all situations. The sermon of the Bhagavad Gita was delivered by Lord Krishna on the battlefield to inspire Arjuna to fight when he was terribly bewildered and, in extreme grief, refused to fight. The sacred text encourages us to bounce back from difficult situations and navigate life with ease.

Devotion to God, Karma Yoga, and Yoga Knowledge are great pillars of the Bhagavad Gita, which offer a clear insight for building resilience by way of understanding life and approaching it with ease of flow. In the Bhagavad Gita, Lord Krishna elucidates that one who follows the paths of Yoga of Knowledge (Gyan Yoga), Yoga of Devotion (Bhakti Yog), and Yoga of Actions (Karma Yoga) remains unaffected by pleasures and pains. Let us see how the wisdom of the Bhagavad Gita helps us build resilience.

- **Equanimity for Resilience**: The Bhagavad Gita offers equanimity as a tool for developing resilience. Equanimity is a state of mental calmness, even in the face of adversity. As discussed earlier in the chapter, the Bhagavad Gita preaches equanimity and also teaches effective techniques for developing it, laying the foundation for resilience.

  Verse 56 of Chapter 2 of the Bhagavad Gita says: "One whose mind remains undisturbed amidst misery, who does not crave pleasure, and who is free from attachment, fear, and anger, is called a sage of steady wisdom."

  Bhagavad Gita 2:56: [https://vivekavani.com/b2v56/]

Verse 20 of Chapter 5 of the Bhagavad Gita says: "A person who neither rejoices upon achieving something pleasant nor laments upon obtaining something unpleasant; who is self-intelligent; who is not bewildered; and who knows the science of God is already situated in transcendence."

Bhagavad Gita 5:20: [https://vivekavani.com/b5v20/]

As discussed earlier in the chapter, equanimity can be developed through meditation and by conquering the mind through practice. Such an enlightened person, who develops a state of equanimity, has great spiritual resilience, and holds out against adversity, trauma, stress, or tragedy, can be stable rapidly.

Verse 7 of Chapter 6 of the Bhagavad Gita states that those who conquer their minds attain tranquility, and they remain equipoise in happiness or distress, heat or cold, and in honor or dishonor.

Bhagavad Gita 6:7: [https://vivekavani.com/b6v7/]

- **Resilience Embedded in Karma Yoga:** The concept of Karma Yoga, as explained earlier in the chapter, holds one's duty above everything. By performing actions in the discharge of our duties without emotions or a feeling of desire, we liberate ourselves from the bondage of the cycles of birth.

In Verse 38 of Chapter 2, Lord Krishna urges Arjuna to fight for the sake of duty, treating alike happiness and distress, loss and gain, and victory and defeat. Lord Krishna assures him that by fulfilling his responsibility in this way, he will never incur sin.

Bhagavad Gita 2:38: [https://vivekavani.com/b2v38/]

It is stated in Verse 57 of Chapter 2 of the Bhagavad Gita that one who remains unattached under all conditions and is neither delighted by good fortune nor dejected by tribulations is a sage with perfect knowledge.

Bhagavad Gita 2:57: [https://vivekavani.com/b2v57/]

Further, Verse 47 of Chapter 2 lays emphasis on the performance of actions without attachment to the results of the actions. And we are not supposed to abandon out of fear of failure, frustration of defeat, or disinterest the actions that we are required to perform as per the duties assigned to us.

Bhagavad Gita 2:47:[https://vivekavani.com/b2v47/]

Thus, by following the wisdom of Karma Yoga, we may develop spiritual resilience, enabling ourselves to remain stable in failure and success, in hours of defeat and victory, and in shame and glory.

- **Faith in God and Resilience:** Faith in God provides inner strength and a sense of purpose in challenging times and promotes a sense of inner power to bounce back from adversity and suffering. By developing spiritual strength and trust in oneself, individuals can bounce back from challenges and adversity with determination and composure. In verse 22 of Chapter 9 of the Bhagavad Gita, Lord Krishna assures His devotees of great love and protection from all types of miseries. In Verse 22 of Chapter 9 of the Bhagavad Gita, Lord Krishna says that to those who always think of Him, engage in exclusive devotion to Him, and whose minds are always absorbed in Him, He provides what they lack and preserves what they already possess.

  Bhagavad Gita 9:22: [https://vivekavani.com/b9v22/]

Further, in Verse 29 of Chapter 9 of the Bhagavad Gita, Lord Krishna says that He is equally disposed to all living beings and is neither inimical nor partial to anyone, but the devotees who worship Him with love reside in Him, and He resides in them.

Bhagavad Gita 9:29: [https://vivekavani.com/b9v29/]

By following the paths of Devotion to God (Bhakti Yoga), Yoga of Actions (Karma Yoga), and Yoga of Knowledge (Gyan Yoga) as preached by the Bhagavad Gita, we develop a clear insight for building resilience. By way of understanding life, we learn to bounce back from adversity and navigate life with ease.

Section 5: Bhagavad Gita for Success in Career and Relationships

1. Belief in Self: Self-belief is a feeling or consciousness of one's capabilities or efforts to accomplish tasks. You would agree that self-belief is essential for living an effective, empowered, and fulfilling life. Self-belief empowers us with the ability to think, speak, and act purposefully. That makes us believe that we have the inherent strength and courage to succeed. The Bhagavad Gita teaches us that by living at the level of higher consciousness and leading a purposeful life, we can realize our capabilities and potential. The sacred text also highlights the importance of practicing meditation for silencing doubts, fear, and anxiety. Let us see how the Bhagavad Gita helps us cultivate self-belief.

- **Realizing our True Self:** When we live from the level of the eternal soul rather than the mortal body, we nurture a unique belief in ourselves, shedding fear, insecurity, and doubt. Our thoughts, speech, and actions embody the essence of a pure, unbounded soul—fearless, confident, and courageous.

In Verse 18 of Chapter 2 of the Bhagavad Gita, Lord Krishna inspires Arjuna to fight without fear by saying that it is the body that perishes, but the soul embedded in the body is indestructible, immeasurable, and eternal.

Bhagavad Gita 2:18:[https://vivekavani.com/b2v18/]

By living from the higher level of the soul, on the one hand, we develop a commitment to ethical values springing from the soul, and on the other hand, we shed all fears and doubts, empowering ourselves to overcome challenges boldly and make a positive impact on the world around us.

- **Living a Purposeful Life**: By understanding the importance of our duties in leading a purposeful life, as preached by the Bhagavad Gita, we feel driven to believe that the task we are performing is meaningful to the world. And by doing so, we cultivate self-belief.

  In Verses 31 to 33 of Chapter 2 of the Bhagavad Gita, Lord Krishna reminds Arjuna that, as a warrior, he must fight for righteousness, and by abandoning his duty, he would bring shame to his name and also incur a sin. He further tells him that for a warrior, there is no better engagement than fighting for righteousness, as it opens for him the gates to celestial abodes.

  Bhagavad Gita 2:31: [https://vivekavani.com/b2v31/]

  Bhagavad Gita 2:32: [https://vivekavani.com/b2v32/]

  Bhagavad Gita 2:33: [https://vivekavani.com/b2v33/]

By committing ourselves to our duty, we become motivated to realize our potential and abilities, leading to a belief in ourselves.

- **Overcoming Selfish Desires:** Self-doubt, worry, guilt, fear, and anxiety rob us of our self-belief. The Bhagavad Gita explains that the cause of these negative emotions is either our attachment to the fruits of our actions or our non-performance of our actions.

As per Verse 48 of Chapter 2 of the Bhagavad Gita, we should not have any attachment to the fruit of our actions, as that breeds desires, which in turn give rise to fear, anxiety, guilt, worry, and other negative emotions; nor should we abandon actions out of fear of shame of failure, frustration of defeat, or disinterest in the actions.

Bhagavad Gita 2:48: [https://vivekavani.com/b2v48/]

By overcoming selfish desires, we avoid negative emotions like fear, anxiety, guilt, and self-doubt, which bog us down. And thus, we cultivate self-belief.

- **Experience builds self-belief.** There is a famous saying: Practice makes a man perfect. When you gain experience, your skills grow, and you become more capable of navigating your activities with skill and ease, nurturing self-belief.

  The Bhagavad Gita places great emphasis on the importance of practice for achieving perfection. In Verse 35 of Chapter 6 of the Bhagavad Gita, Lord Krishna says that the mind is indeed very difficult to restrain, but with practice and detachment, it can be controlled.

  Bhagavad Gita6:35: [https://vivekavani.com/b6v35/]

- **Meditation for Self-Belief**: The Bhagavad Gita preaches that the voices of doubt, indecision, fear, and anxiety can be silenced through the practice of meditation. Besides, meditation allows us to have a direct experience of our soul—the infinite, immortal, unbounded, pure spirit.

Verse 15 of Chapter 6 of the Bhagavad Gita says: "Through meditation, one can quiet the restless mind, connect with the true self, and attain liberation from the cycle of rebirth."

Bhagavad Gita 6:15: [https://vivekavani.com/b6v15/]

Meditation is a path of self-realization and union with the divine. By practicing meditation, we cultivate physical and mental discipline, leading to inner peace and strength and developing self-belief.

In conclusion, self-belief is essential for living an effective and empowered life in a fulfilled manner. As preached by the Bhagavad Gita, we may cultivate self-belief by living life from the level of the eternal soul, leading a purposeful life, overcoming our selfish desires, practicing meditation, and sharpening our skills and know-how with experience.

2. Effective Communication:

Effective communication is not only crucial for building strong relationships but also essential for effective leadership. The Bhagavad Gita, through Lord Krishna's teachings to Arjuna, acknowledges the power of communication as a means to inspire, guide, and uplift others.

In the sermon of the Bhagavad Gita, clear and meaningful communication is exemplified in the way Lord Krishna imparts wisdom to Arjuna. Lord Krishna delivers the sermon with compassion and understanding, establishing a strong connection with Arjuna's heart and mind.

The sacred text emphasizes the importance of active listening as an integral part of effective communication. By genuinely paying attention to others, we create an environment of trust and empathy, making them feel valued and understood. This fosters a deeper connection and paves the way for open and honest dialogue.

The Bhagavad Gita encourages individuals to establish a genuine connection with their audience. Whether it is in personal relationships or leadership roles, effective communication involves tailoring the message to resonate with the audience's needs and emotions. By understanding their perspectives and concerns, we can effectively address their needs and inspire them to take positive action.

The Bhagavad Gita also underscores the significance of humility and respect in communication. When we approach others with humility and treat them with respect, we create a positive and harmonious atmosphere for effective communication. This paves the way for constructive discussions and collaborative problem-solving.

The Bhagavad Gita emphasizes the importance of self-introspection, which is a crucial prerequisite for effective communication. By understanding our thoughts and emotions, we can communicate more authentically and empathetically. When we are mindful of our words and intentions, our communication becomes more meaningful and impactful.

The conversation in the Bhagavad Gita between Lord Krishna and Arjuna highlights the significance of clarity and balance in language. By choosing our words carefully, we can avoid misunderstandings and hurtful exchanges. Honest and kind communication fosters healthy relationships and promotes a harmonious social environment.

In conclusion, the Bhagavad Gita serves as a timeless guide for developing effective communication skills. By learning from Lord Krishna's example, we can cultivate the art of connecting with others through clear and meaningful communication, active listening, and genuine empathy. As we apply these principles in our personal and professional interactions, we can build strong relationships, inspire others, and create a positive impact on the world around us.

3. **Relationship Harmony through the Bhagavad Gita**

Creating and maintaining healthy relationships is essential for personal growth, happiness, and overall well-being. Let us see how the teachings of the Bhagavad Gita provide us with profound wisdom and guidance to foster relationship harmony.

- **Realistic Expectations:** The Bhagavad Gita encourages us to have realistic expectations in our relationships. By understanding the impermanence of the material world and recognizing the eternal nature of the soul, we reduce expectations of perfection from others. This understanding helps us embrace the uniqueness of each individual, fostering acceptance and harmony in our relationships.

- **Effective Communication:** Effective communication is the cornerstone of healthy relationships. The Bhagavad Gita is a classical example of truthful and compassionate communication. When we communicate honestly and with empathy, we build trust and understanding with others.

- **Dependability:** Dependability is a quality highly valued in any relationship. The Bhagavad Gita teaches us the significance of being dependable by fulfilling our duties and responsibilities with sincerity and dedication. When we can be relied upon by others, our relationships grow stronger.

- **Balance:** Finding balance in life is essential for maintaining healthy relationships. The Bhagavad Gita guides us in leading a life of moderation and self-control. When we maintain balance in our actions and desires, we are better equipped to nurture our relationships without becoming overwhelmed.

4. **Seeking Wise Counsel**

The Bhagavad Gita serves as a classical example of guidance and counseling that one should seek when faced with bewilderment. Of course, clear communication and active listening are crucial aspects of meaningful counseling.

When Arjuna faces a dilemma on the battlefield and refuses to fight with his kin and teacher, Lord Krishna serves as a divine counselor to him, providing him with wisdom and clarity. Realizing that he is too bewildered to think about what should be done and what should not be done, Arjuna asks Lord Krishna to guide him. While seeking counsel from Lord Krishna, Arjuna calls himself His disciple, surrenders to Him, and asks Him to advise what is in his best interest.

In Verse 7 of Chapter 2 of the Bhagavad Gita, Arjuna humbly says to Lord Krishna, "I am confused about my duty and am besieged with anxiety and faint-heartedness. I am your disciple, and I have surrendered to you. Please instruct me on what is best for me."

Bhagavad Gita2:7: [https://vivekavani.com/b2v7/]

Further, in Verse 8 of Chapter 2 of the Bhagavad Gita, Arjuna says to Lord Krishna, "I can find no means of driving away this anguish that is drying up my senses. Even if I win a prosperous and unrivaled kingdom on earth or gain sovereignty like the celestial gods, I will be unable to dispel this grief."

Bhagavad Gita 2:8: [https://vivekavani.com/b2v8/]

During the sermon of the Bhagavad Gita, whenever doubt crops in Arjuna's mind, he does not hesitate to request Lord Krishna to dispel his doubts.

In Verses 1 to 2 of Chapter 3 of the Bhagavad Gita, Arjuna tells Lord Krishna that his intellect is bewildered and asks Him why He preaches him to fight if He considers that knowledge is superior to action. He further asks Him to tell him decisively the one path by which he may attain the highest good.

Bhagavad Gita 3:2: [https://vivekavani.com/b3v2/]

Arjuna, from time to time, seeks clarifications from Lord Krishna over various subjects such as the Absolute Truth, the soul, renunciation, and forces impelling sinful acts.

There is often a situation in our lives when we also face a dilemma or challenge, as Arjuna faced. Under such circumstances, one's intellect is clouded, and one is unable to determine what is right or wrong. Under such circumstances, the wrong decisions may prove catastrophic. In moments of confusion, dilemma, or bewilderment, it is advisable to seek counsel for a future course of action from a learned friend, relative, or well-wisher rather than suffer due to a bad decision. By seeking wise counsel, we gain new perspectives and make informed decisions, avoiding confusion and uncertainty. Let us learn from Arjuna the art of taking counsel and adding happiness to our lives.

Personal Experiences: As we have learned, the teachings of the Bhagavad Gita touch all aspects of life. The teachings not only inspire us to inculcate essential qualities for success in career and relationships, a stress-free and healthy life, but also guide us on how we can do so to fill our lives with blissfulness. Overcoming sensual desires, devotion to God, and selfless performance of actions are cornerstones of the Bhagavad Gita.

The teachings of the sacred book touched my mind and soul early in my childhood. I completely surrendered myself to God, believing in His presence at the center of this universe. Though I was overwhelmed by the wisdom in the teachings of the Bhagavad Gita, I consciously started aligning my actions with the deeper core values embedded in its teachings a bit late. The teachings of the sacred book helped me lead an authentic life, make crucial decisions prudently, and maintain a compassionate outlook. Overcoming sensual desires is a difficult task, but with purification of mind and practice, we can control our senses. It is a lifelong process. If I look back, a lot has been achieved in this direction, but still, the task is not over. Had I followed the teachings of the Bhagavad Gita in letter and spirit right from my adolescent days, I would have tackled a few difficult situations in life in a much more magnanimous manner. I strongly believe that introducing the teachings of the Bhagavad Gita as a compulsory subject in academic curricula at the school level can foster the development of well-rounded individuals with exceptional qualities, encompassing both intellect and compassion and nurturing a nationalistic outlook.

In conclusion, the Bhagavad Gita offers timeless wisdom and practical guidance for living a meaningful and purposeful life. By integrating its teachings into our daily practices and striving to live by its principles, we can experience personal growth, spiritual development, and positive transformations in various aspects of life. Embracing the teachings of the Bhagavad Gita can lead to a more enlightened and harmonious existence, benefiting both individuals and society at large.

In the following chapter, 'Living with Purpose: A Blueprint for Fulfillment', we will delve deeper into the practical applications of the teachings of the Bhagavad Gita for laying a healthy foundation to live and thrive into aging. We would endeavor to craft a blueprint that aims at achieving success in careers and relationships while nurturing physical health and mental wellness. The teachings of the Bhagavad Gita provide profound insights into nurturing a meaningful and fulfilling life. Let us move forward to craft the blueprint for living a long and happy life.

CHAPTER-5

Living with Purpose: Crafting a Blueprint for Fulfillment

Introduction: Have you at any stage of life consciously or subconsciously contemplated the idea of crafting a blueprint for your life? If so, what were the key elements? And if not, do you feel that you should have done so? The importance of crafting a blueprint for life may be found in the answers to these questions, whatever they may be.

Life is a journey filled with opportunities and choices, and each decision we make shapes our path and defines our experiences. There are also challenges from time to time. In this chapter, we explore the significance of creating a life mission and vision and how aligning our actions with our core values can lead to a life filled with fulfillment and happiness. We would delve into the art of living actively with purpose and intention. We would discuss the most important choices in life we need to make at appropriate times. The aim of drafting a blueprint for life is to ascertain what you need to do and how to do it so that it makes you happy and helps you live longer. The book attempts to set you on a path to taking actions that will provide long-term benefits. The focus would be on creating coherence in the physical, mental, spiritual, and emotional realms to lay the foundation for blissful aging beyond 100.

The importance of drafting the blueprint of life is reflected in the words of John C. Maxwell: The timing of your decision is just as important as the decision you make.[9]

---

[9]John C. Maxwell: Inspirational, Decisions You Make, and Important

Section 1: Crafting Your Life's Mission and Vision

1. Importance of Crafting a Blueprint for Life: Life is more than just short-term goals; it's about having a clear sense of direction and purpose. By creating a life mission and vision statement, we gain clarity about our overarching goals and aspirations. This blueprint becomes our guide, providing direction and alignment for every decision we make.

John C. Maxwell once rightly said: "We need to make a few critical decisions in major areas of our life and then manage those decisions day to day."[10]

2. Crafting a Blueprint for a Meaningful Life: It is easy to choose a path of anonymity and lead an empty life, but striving and leading an impactful life requires a burning desire to realize our dreams. Mahatma Gandhi inspired us to live our lives with intention, meaning, and purpose by asking the question, "What is in our life's blueprint?" You would agree that self-worth, ambition to achieve excellence, commitment to duty, and deep core values should be essential elements in the blueprint for a fulfilled life. To contribute to the world and achieve greatness, we must have self-belief. That belief comes from within, not from external validation. By engaging in activities that make us proud, we can develop a sense of self-worth. Determination to achieve excellence comes from passion, and when the blueprint for your life reflects your determination to achieve excellence, nothing can stop you. Thomas Alva Edison's relentless pursuit of innovation and invention showcases the power of having a vision and working towards it with determination.

---

[10]John C. Maxwell (2011), "The 360-Degree Leader with Workbook: Developing Your Influence from Anywhere in the Organization," p. 85, Thomas Nelson Inc.

Emphasizing the importance of crafting a blueprint of life that imbues an ambition to achieve excellence, the American host and television producer, Oprah Winfrey, once said, "Create the highest, grandest vision possible for your life, because you become what you believe."[11]

You would agree that commitment to duty has a great driving force that keeps you on track. When the blueprint of your life resonates with a commitment to duty, love, and justice, you choose to live a life for a higher cause. Understanding what truly matters to us inspires us to live authentically and make decisions that resonate with our deepest desires and beliefs. By investing in the structure of our lives with a solid blueprint based on core principles, we can find inner strength and bring greater meaning and well-being to our lives. Mahatma Gandhi, with his unwavering commitment to non-violence and justice, serves as an inspiration for living a life guided by higher principles.

John C. Maxwell very rightly described the importance of commitment to the core values by saying, "Commitment is the first step to every good thing I know and the only step that matters when it comes to achievement. It inspires and attracts people, shows them you have conviction and goals, and that you are focused and determined. And the commitment that is based on values will endure. Any time you make choices based on solid life values, you are in a better position to sustain your level of commitment because you don't have to continually re-evaluate its importance."[12]

---

[11]Oprah Winfrey, Janet Lowe (1998) "Oprah Winfrey speaks: insight from the world's most influential voice," John Wiley & Sons. https://www.azquotes.com/author/15820-Oprah_Winfrey

[12]Facebook post by John C. Maxwell from September 25, 2014

The blueprint for a fulfilled life should reflect an intention to achieve excellence and a passion to achieve the goals of life.

Emphasizing the importance of intention in achieving excellence in life, the great philosopher and political and spiritual thinker Aristotle said, "Excellence is never an accident. It is always the result of high intention, sincere effort, and intelligent execution; it represents the wise choice of many alternatives; choice not chance, determines your destiny."

Section 2: Navigating Key Decisions in Adulthood

As we transition into adulthood, we are faced with new opportunities for growth and self-understanding. That is a crucial period for making key decisions that lay the foundation for a fulfilled life. We are challenged to seek answers and make unique choices that promote our well-being as individuals.

The choices of a career and a life partner are among the most significant decisions that you make in the early phase of life. Undoubtedly, they lay the foundation for the rest of life. That makes it very important that these vital life decisions are taken very carefully, keeping in mind your likes and dislikes, core values, and commitments.

Let us understand the importance of various vital decisions taken in the early years of life:

1. Selection of Career: In the present-day world of technology, there is cutthroat competition in various fields, making career selection with due consideration to aptitude and interest more critical than ever before. By understanding our values and interests, we can determine which career options align with our happiness and fulfillment.

Dr. Abdul Kalam's passion for science and his unwavering commitment to education serve as a powerful example of aligning one's career with one's passions and values.

Thomas Alva Edison was asked to leave the school, but his passion for science and research made him the greatest inventor of all time. Also, the role played by his mother in keeping his spirits alive underscores the role of parenting in the career of the children.

Brian Tracy, motivational speaker and author, once rightly said, "If you raise your children to feel that they can accomplish any goal or task they decide upon, you will have succeeded as a parent, and you will have given your children the greatest of all blessings."

John C. Maxwell confirms the importance of discipline and goal-setting in the selection of a career by saying, "Decision-making takes care of goal-setting, but discipline also takes care of goal-getting. Decisions and discipline can't be separated; one is worthless without the other."

2. Choice of Life Partner: Choosing a life partner is a decision that impacts every area of life. Finding the right person can be a monumental task, but by having a realistic idea of the kind of person who is right for you, making a strong effort to find him or her, and committing fully to the relationship, you can share your life with someone you love.

Tips for Selecting a Life Partner: You need to have clarity of mind about the life partner of your dreams. That helps you make the right choice, laying the foundation for a fulfilled married life.

Tony Robbins has rightly said, "When you know what is most important to you, making a decision is quite simple."[13]

Young adults may keep the following tips in mind while choosing a life partner:

a) **Understand Your Values and Priorities**: Take time to identify your core values and what you prioritize in a life partner. Consider qualities such as kindness, honesty, compatibility, and shared interests. Knowing what truly matters to you will guide you in finding a partner who aligns with your values.

b) **Communicate openly and honestly.** Effective communication is essential in any relationship. Be open and honest about your feelings, expectations, and aspirations. Create a safe space for your potential partner to share their thoughts as well. Transparent communication builds trust and understanding.

c) **Observe their characters.** Pay attention to how a person behaves, treats others, and handles challenges. Look for qualities like empathy, respect, and emotional intelligence. A partner with strong character traits will contribute positively to the relationship's growth and harmony.

d) **Assess Compatibility and Shared Goals:** Evaluate whether your potential partner's long-term goals and aspirations align with yours. Compatibility in areas like lifestyle, family, and plans is crucial for a successful and fulfilling partnership.

e) **Mutual Respect and Support**: A healthy relationship is built on mutual respect and support. Ensure that your partner

---

[13]Tony Robbins (2012), "Awaken the Giant Within," p. 400, Simon and Schuster

respects your individuality and supports your personal growth and endeavors. Likewise, be willing to offer the same respect and support in return.

f) **Trust your instincts.** While considering logical factors is essential, don't ignore your instincts and intuition. Sometimes, your gut feelings can offer valuable insights about the suitability of a potential partner.

Personal Experiences: Let me share with you my own experiences regarding the selection of a career and life partner. My academic record in school was brilliant. I had in mind many career proposals that were propelled by high ambitions rather than aptitude or interest. There was neither an aptitude test nor any career counseling to decide which career I should choose. On the day of admission to the engineering college, I was clueless about the branch of engineering I should opt for. I believe that the holistic personality development of the child is very important so that he moves on from one stage to another with flow.

As regards the selection of a life partner, I had a lot of clarity in my mind. I wanted my wife to be a government college lecturer, pretty, and have a belief in spiritual values. Though it was not an easy affair those days to find a partner of that sort, I didn't give into social pressures and ultimately found the life partner of my dreams after spirited efforts. I believe that once you choose a life partner based on your deep core values, your fondness for them doesn't fade despite differences of opinion on minor issues, and there is no difficulty in arriving at a consensus on major issues of great value for the family, which is very important for a happy married life.

3. Everyday Actions for a Happier, Longer Life:

a) **Prioritizing Physical and Mental Health:** In the blueprint of life, health occupies the center stage. Aging begins around the age of 30, and staying physically active becomes the key to slowing down the aging process. Health is not a goal to be achieved, and that is done. Have you ever observed that once you are irregular in your workouts or are negligent about your diet, unhealthy symptoms take no time to appear? You ought to understand that living a healthy and long life is a journey that starts in adolescence and continues throughout life.

   We would discuss in Chapter 6: Nurturing Physical Vitality: The Foundation of Lasting Bliss, the various benefits of physical activity, the options available, and why it is important to nurture physical well-being throughout the adult years for blissful aging beyond 100.

b) **Developing a Taste for Nourishment:** A healthy diet rich in nutrients is equally important for physical fitness and mental wellness. Rather than viewing food as mere indulgence, we should recognize it as a means of nourishing and healing our bodies. Developing a taste for nutritious food is crucial, as our food habits become ingrained over time. Embracing a healthful perspective on food is transformative for our well-being.

   Former President of the USA, Horace Mann, beautifully described the significance of developing a taste for nourishing food by saying, "Healthy eating is a way of life, so it is important to establish routines that are simple, realistic, and ultimately liveable."

   The importance of a nourishing diet will be discussed in detail in Chapter 6: Nurturing Physical Vitality: The Foundation of Lasting Bliss.

c) **Learning a Lesson from the Lifestyle of the Centenarians of Okinawa:** Meanwhile, let us have a look at the report of the World Economic Forum on the secrets to the longevity of the people of Okinawa, a town in Japan.

Japan has a record-high number of centenarians, people who are 100 or more. Okinawa, an island in the Kyushu region of the country, is regarded as a blue zone because it has a large number of people living above 100. It is almost twice as common for Okinawans to live beyond 100 years as it is in all of Japan. Here's how they live longer:

i) **Living with Purpose (Ikigai):** The secret to the longer life of Japanese centenarians is Ikigai, living with a purpose. Let us have a look at the list of tips and advice prepared by the World Economic Forum in a survey of these people on how to live life with maximum efficiency.

ii) **Diet:** According to Dr. Bradley Willcox, who authored the book The Okinawan Way, the centenarians include a lot of fruits, vegetables, and legumes in their daily diet.

iii) **Hara Hachi Bu:** It is a form of practice that the Okinawans follow. According to this, you are only supposed to eat to a point where you are 80 percent full.

iv) **Staying Mentally Engaged:** Okinawans do not believe in retirement. People are quite open about what they want to do and focus on things that they love doing. "I think the Okinawan concept is just to stay engaged, and I think that helps them a lot. I think it also contributes to decreasing the cost of health care," said Dr. Willcox.

v) **Social Group:** Large families and strong support groups are other factors that add years to the lives of Okinawans. People join Moais, or social groups, where they meet, drink tea, and discuss news and other happenings around them.

vi) **Relationship with Time:** According to Dr. Willcox, the Okinawans have a "slower sense of time." Rather than running after deadlines and getting consumed with work, Okinawans prefer to take it easy.

vii) **Spirituality:** Spirituality is the relationship between the body, mind, and soul, to which Okinawans give utmost priority. They focus on maintaining a healthy ecosystem within and outside their bodies.

Let us draw inspiration from the people of Okinawa to chalk out our daily lifestyle for 100 years of happiness.

Section 3: The Blueprint for Life Beyond 100

As we lay down the blueprint for the later chapters of our lives, we are crafting a symphony that blends the art of living with the science of aging. Our choices today are the brushstrokes that shape our journey through the years to come. Every facet of our well-being, whether physical, mental, or emotional, intertwines to compose a life imbued with joy and fulfillment. The wisdom we've gathered, the connections we've nurtured, and the purpose we've unearthed contribute to a life well lived. We are not merely aging gracefully; we are thriving, embracing the passage of time with grace, gratitude, and unwavering enthusiasm. This adventure beckons us to savor each moment, invest in our health and growth, and craft a life beyond 100 that radiates vibrancy, purpose, and profound fulfillment. Before moving forward, let us have a look at the two most distinguished centenarians: Goodenough, the oldest recipient of the Nobel Prize at the age of 97, and Calyampudi Radhakrishan Rao, who was awarded the International Prize in Statistics at the age of 102.

Nobel laureate John B. Goodenough, the pioneer of the development of lithium-ion batteries that are used in millions of electric vehicles all around the world, died on June 25, 2023, at the age of 100. Goodenough received the 2019 Nobel Prize for Chemistry, along with Britain's Stanley Whittingham and Japan's Akira Yoshino, for their respective research into lithium-ion batteries, making him the oldest recipient of a Nobel Prize. He was born on July 25, 1922, in Jena, Germany, to American parents. He and his wife were married for over 70 years until she died in 2016. In the recent past, before his death, Goodenough and his university team had been working on exploring new directions for energy storage, including a "glass" battery with a solid-state electrolyte and lithium or sodium metal electrodes.

Calyampudi Radhakrishan Rao was awarded the International Prize in Statistics at the age of 102, which recognized Rao's works and their applications in such diverse fields as anthropology, biology, social sciences, psychology, and national planning. Rao's research in multivariate analysis has been used in economic planning, weather prediction, medical diagnosis, tracking the movements of spy planes, and monitoring the course of spacecraft. Calyampudi R. Rao, who was born on September 10, 1920, to Telgu parents in Hadagali Village in the Bellary District of Karnataka in India, died on June 25, 2023, at the age of 103. He was married in 1948 to Bharghavi, who died at the age of 92. Calyampudi R. Rao went to the US after retirement at 60, when most Indian elders go to America for a leisure trip. He was invited to join the statistics faculty at the University of Pittsburgh at the age of 62. Eventually, he went on to chair the department at Pennsylvania State University at 70 and became a US citizen in 1995 at 75. At 82, he was recognized by the White House for his contribution to the world of statistics and awarded the National Medal for Science in 2002.

Of course, the lives of Goodenough and Calyampudi R. Rao would be a North Star compass for all those who aspire to live meaningfully, a fulfilled life beyond 100. There are two common things one can notice in the lives of the two outstanding centenarians: a long married life and an incessant zeal to accomplish their mission without any consideration of age.

1. Embracing the Journey of Transformation

As we set foot on the path of life, we must acknowledge that aging is not a single event but an ongoing evolution. While its pace may vary, the fifties and sixties mark the prelude to this transformative odyssey, with its momentum gaining momentum in the seventies. During this voyage, nearly every aspect of our being changes. Among these shifts, our brain and musculoskeletal system bear witness to some of the most profound effects. Ideally, you might have been practicing healthy habits throughout your life. But even if you haven't, it's never too late to start taking proactive steps to maintain and improve your health. Small lifestyle changes can have a big impact. They can help you prevent or better manage chronic diseases, and keep your body fit, and your brain sharp. Adopting even a few of the habits listed here will start you on the right track for healthy aging.

2. Staying Physically Active for a Healthy Body

a) **Mental Wellness**: Mental health emerges as a vital frontier as the years unfold. Globally, Alzheimer's and other brain-related ailments are projected to affect the lives of one in five individuals at some juncture, presenting a significant challenge. Yet, the heartening truth is that diminishing brain health and cognitive function are not inevitable aspects of aging. By embracing physical activity and nurturing positive thought patterns, we not only retain our mental agility but also possess the potential to reverse the aging effects on our minds.

b) **Physical Health**: The passage of time leaves its mark on our cardiovascular system. The heart's muscles may weaken, the artery walls may become less supple, and occasional electrical hitches may disrupt its rhythm. These transformations can lead to reduced blood supply to our organs and breathlessness, even during moderate exertion. Prioritizing cardiovascular health through regular exercise, a balanced diet, stress management, and adequate sleep becomes pivotal in sustaining heart health and staving off risks such as hypertension and stroke.

c) **Nurturing Physical Vitality for Mind and Body:** Exercise can help offset many of the effects of aging. According to Medline Plus, exercising regularly can improve your balance, help keep you mobile, improve your mood by reducing feelings of anxiety and depression, and contribute to better cognitive functioning. It's also an important part of managing and potentially reducing your risk of diseases like diabetes, heart disease, high blood pressure, breast and colon cancer, and osteoporosis.

Any exercise at all is better than none for healthy aging, says the Centers for Disease Control and Prevention (CDC), which recommends 150 minutes of moderate-intensity aerobic activity (like swimming or taking a brisk walk) each week; you can further break this down into 30 active minutes a day for five days a week. It also recommends twice-weekly muscle-strengthening activities. Engaging in consistent physical activity not only bolsters our musculoskeletal health but also supports our heart and brain, enhancing blood circulation and ensuring rejuvenating sleep.

3. Regular Checkups for Holistic Well-Being: The march of time extends its touch to various corners of our body, affecting bladder control, skin resilience, visual and auditory acuity, muscular strength, and even the potency of our immune system. As we embrace longevity, comprehending these changes and taking proactive measures becomes paramount. Regular checkups with your doctor, dentist, eye doctor, and specialist healthcare providers are opportunities to catch problems early and treat them before they become bigger problems.

If you have one or more chronic medical conditions, take multiple medications, are experiencing memory or mobility issues, or have recently been hospitalized, you may want to schedule an appointment with a geriatrician.

4. Fostering Connections for a Purpose-Driven Journey:

The convergence of physical and mental well-being with spiritual growth and social connection forms a cornerstone of blissful aging. A life infused with purpose and engagement becomes our armor against the effects of time. The transition to retirement unfurls new avenues for exploration. Whether through creative pursuits, mentoring, volunteering, or embarking on a new career, each venture enriches the tapestry of our lives. Making the effort to interact with family and friends can have numerous benefits for your health as you age. One article found that participants (all aged 65 and older) who reported higher levels of social activity were more likely to experience more positive moods, fewer negative feelings, and higher levels of physical activity.

If you don't have an active social life, look for opportunities to reconnect with old friends or make new ones. Seek out like-minded others in volunteer activities, gyms, alumni groups, or any other group that corresponds to an interest of yours.

If you're in your sixties or beyond, friendships aren't just the social glue and glitz of life. As you get older, good friendships can dispel loneliness, improve your health, boost your sense of well-being, and even add to your years.[14]

5. Healthy and Balanced Diet:

To get the nutrition your body needs for healthy aging and lower your risk of chronic conditions such as heart disease, make whole foods that are high in fiber and low in saturated fat the foundation of your diet. Following an eating plan like the Mediterranean diet or a similar diet can help you achieve that goal. The Mediterranean diet emphasizes a balance of olive oil, nuts, seeds, fruit and vegetables, whole grains, legumes, and fish. It's low in red meat, full-fat dairy products, and processed foods. You will find more details about the Mediterranean diet in the next chapter.

6. Personalized Health Stewardship:

In the grand tapestry of blissful aging, personalized health management takes center stage. A holistic approach, encompassing regular medical check-ups, a balanced diet, quality sleep, and restricted tobacco and alcohol consumption, forms the bedrock of robust health. Gums, teeth, and specialized medical considerations demand attention, too, as they intricately intertwine with our overall well-being.

---

[14]Kathleen Doheny, "The Healing Power of Friendship Grows with Age," Medically reviewed by Justin Laube (Everyday Health, Reviewed: April 26, 2019)

7. Embracing the Unfolding Chapters:

In the symphony of life, the pursuit of blissful aging emerges as a chapter that beckons with promise. It is a chapter defined not by resignation to the passage of time but by the audacity to infuse each moment with vitality, purpose, and joy. As we stand at the crossroads of experience and anticipation, let us remember that the secrets to enduring well-being are etched within us. The journey toward 100 years of happiness unfolds not merely as a distant aspiration but as a reality that invites us to engage, enrich, and embrace life's every chapter.

Conclusion: Life's blueprint is an ever-evolving work of art that allows us to design a life of purpose, passion, and fulfillment. By making conscious decisions, aligning with our core values, and embracing positive lifestyle choices, we can lead a life that inspires happiness not only for ourselves but also for those whose lives we touch. Let us celebrate the joy of living fully, embracing each moment with gratitude and contentment, leading to a century of fulfillment and happiness.

CHAPTER-6

Nurturing Physical Vitality: The Foundation of Lasting Bliss

Introduction: In this chapter, we delve into the importance of physical health and its role in fostering a blissful and fulfilling life. Our bodies are miraculous vessels that carry us through our journey, and by prioritizing our physical well-being, we can unlock the key to vitality, longevity, and a joyful existence. Let us discover the transformative power of embracing a healthy lifestyle, from nourishing our body with wholesome foods to engaging in regular exercise. Emphasizing the importance of physical health, John F. Kennedy, President of the USA, very rightly observed: Physical fitness is not only one of the most important keys to a healthy body; it is the basis of dynamic and creative intellectual activity.

The relationship between the soundness of the body and the activities of the mind is subtle and complex. Much is not yet understood. But we do know what the Greeks knew: that intelligence and skill can only function at the peak of their capacity when the body is healthy and strong, and that hardy spirits and tough minds usually inhabit sound gods.[15]

Section 1: Embracing an Active Lifestyle

Twin studies have estimated that approximately 20–30% of the variation in human lifespan can be related to **genetics**, with the

---

[15]Sport at the New Frontier: The Soft American". Sports Illustrated, Volume 13, Issue 26, pp. 14–17, December 26, 1960

rest due to individual behaviors and environmental factors which can be modified.[16]

A 2012 study found that even modest amounts of leisure time physical exercise can extend life expectancy by as much as 4.5 years.[17]

1. Unleashing the Benefits of Exercise

- Exploring how physical activity boosts overall health, strengthens the body, enhances your mood, and improves cognitive function

- Finding Your Fitness Passion: Discover various forms of exercise, from cardiovascular workouts to strength training and flexibility exercises, and find the activities that resonate with your interests and abilities.

- Designing a Balanced Exercise Routine: Learn how to create a well-rounded exercise regimen that includes aerobic activities, strength-building exercises, and flexibility training to optimize your physical health.

- **Fueling Your Body for Optimal Health:** Understand the profound impact that nutrition has on your well-being, from providing essential nutrients to fueling your body's functions.

---

[16]vB Hjelmborg J, Iachine I, Skytthe A, Vaupel JW, McGue M, Koskenvuo M, et al. (April 2006), "Genetic influence on human lifespan and longevity," Human Genetics, 119 (3):312–321. DOI:10.1007/s00439-006-0144-PMID-16463022.S2CID8470835.

[17]Moore SC, Patel AV, Matthews CE, Berrington de Gonzalez A, Park Y, Katki HA, et al. (2012) " Leisure time physical activity of moderate to vigorous intensity and mortality: a large pooled cohort analysis." PLOS Medicine 9(11): e1001335. DOI: 10.1371/journal.pmed.1001335,PMC 3491006.PMID, 23139642.

- Building a Balanced Plate: Explore the components of a healthy diet, including whole grains, lean proteins, colorful fruits and vegetables, and healthy fats.

- Mindful Eating: Cultivate a deeper connection with your food, savoring each bite, and nourish your body with intention and gratitude.

- Hydration and Its Role in Vitality: Discover the importance of staying hydrated and how proper hydration supports various bodily functions and promotes overall health.

2. Incredible Benefits of Exercise

Exercise and physical activity offer numerous benefits that can positively impact our lives in ways we might not have imagined. Physical activity is not just a means to feel better; that is the key to:

a) **Boosting Health:** Regardless of age, sex, or physical ability, everyone stands to benefit from incorporating exercise into their daily routine. As per the WHO Report on Physical Activity published on October 5, 2023, people who are insufficiently active have a 20% to 30% increased risk of death compared to people who are sufficiently active. The report says that physical activity contributes to preventing and managing non-communicable diseases such as cardiovascular diseases, cancer, and diabetes and reduces symptoms of depression and anxiety. According to the American Heart Association (last reviewed: November 1, 2021), healthy adults should engage in at least 150 minutes of moderate aerobic activity and 75 minutes of vigorous aerobic activity each week, or a combination of both. Activities like running, walking, and swimming are excellent choices. Strength training exercises for all major muscle groups should also be performed at least two times a week. Ideally, these activities may be spread throughout the week.

b) **Weight Management:** Exercise plays a pivotal role in maintaining a healthy weight. It helps prevent excess weight gain, assists in weight maintenance, and promotes weight loss. When engaging in physical activity, calories are burned, and weight control becomes more manageable. Effective weight management combines exercise with a balanced diet.

c) **Improving Mood:** Exercise triggers the production of endorphins and enkephalins, hormones responsible for feelings of happiness, relaxation, and pleasure. It helps shift our focus away from negative thoughts, leading to emotional relief and increased well-being.

d) **Boosting Energy:** Regular physical activity enhances muscle strength and endurance, leading to improved cardiovascular health and increased energy levels for daily tasks.

e) **Promoting Better Sleep:** Engaging in regular physical activity can help individuals fall asleep faster, experience better quality sleep, and wake up feeling more refreshed.

f) **Enhancing Sex Life:** Exercise can boost energy levels, increase confidence in physical appearance, and may enhance arousal in women. Men who exercise regularly are less likely to experience erectile dysfunction.

g) **Having Fun**: Exercise and physical activity can be enjoyable, providing opportunities to unwind, connect with nature, or participate in activities that bring joy. They also serve as an excellent means of socializing and bonding with family and friends.

h) **Combating Health Conditions and Diseases**: Regular exercise offers a range of health benefits, including:

i) **Cardiovascular Health**: It boosts "good" HDL cholesterol, reduces unhealthy triglycerides, and keeps blood flowing smoothly, decreasing the risk of cardiovascular diseases.

j) **Preventing and Managing Health Concerns**: Physical activity helps prevent or manage conditions such as stroke, metabolic syndrome, high blood pressure, type 2 diabetes, depression, anxiety, certain cancers, arthritis, and falls. It also improves cognitive function and reduces the risk of death from all causes. The implementation of daily physical activity and exercise prevention interventions supports an 80% reduction in CVD risk, a 90% reduction in type 2 diabetes risk, a 33% reduction in cancer risk, and, in some cases, reductions in all-cause mortality.[18]

Incorporating exercise into your daily routine can truly transform your life. Whether it's a brisk walk, a swim, a jog, or participation in sports, staying active offers a multitude of physical, mental, and emotional benefits. It's a key component of a healthy and vibrant lifestyle.

Personal Experiences: Let me share with you my experiences about remaining physically fit. At the time of passing out of the engineering college, I was underweight and looked lanky. Within a few months of dedicated efforts, I gained the desired

---

[18]Durstine, J. Larry. "Physical activity, exercise, and chronic diseases: A brief review." Sports Medicine and Health Science (SMHS) Journal, Department of Exercise Science, University of South Carolina, Columbia, SC, USA Published on December 26, 2019

weight and an attractive physique. Thereafter, I hardly missed a walk in the morning or swimming in the evening. With a balanced diet in mind, I have consciously developed my taste buds for healthy foods to my liking. I am careful about my weight management and try to keep my body mass index (BMI) consistently around 24. The benefits are healthy biorhythms, sound sleep, and a good appetite. The BP levels have improved to 115/75. If you choose an exercise or a sport intelligently as per your interests, it not only boosts physical health but also considerably improves your cognitive functions. It is also a great source of joy and provides you with a platform for socializing. I decided in my early forties to go for swimming regularly with my wife. In the first season of swimming, both of us lost weight miraculously, with our physiques getting remarkably improved, and there was a great feeling of rejuvenation. That swimming season was so thrilling that we became accustomed to this evening routine. I have also been regularly going for a morning walk of around 6 kilometers for the last 30 years. In Chandigarh, Sukhna Lake, Rose Garden, Leisure Valley, Bougainville Garden, and various parks are wonderful places with different types of terrain. We visit these places in rotation to avail ourselves of the benefits of different terrains for muscle-strengthening. I find profound joy in clicking photos of mesmerizing nature during my morning walks. There are many options available for keeping ourselves physically active while making our daily routine joyful. The point is to make a smart choice about the physical activity that you may follow religiously. By aligning our exercise routine with our interests and capabilities, we remain committed to regular exercise. We also need to understand the importance of tailoring exercise to our individual fitness levels and health conditions.

Of course, before starting a new exercise program, it is always advisable to consult with a doctor, especially if there are concerns about fitness levels or chronic health conditions.

Section 2: Embracing a Balanced and Nourishing Diet: Fueling Your Body for Optimal Health

Incorporating a balanced and healthy diet is equally crucial to complementing the benefits of exercise. A balanced diet provides adequate calories, proteins, minerals, vitamins, and other essential nutrients. Additionally, it includes bioactive phytochemicals like dietary fiber, antioxidants, and nutraceuticals, which contribute to positive health outcomes.

1. Embracing a Balanced Diet

A balanced diet is one that incorporates various types of foods in specific quantities and proportions and meets the body's requirements for calories, proteins, minerals, vitamins, and other essential nutrients. A well-balanced diet not only provides the necessary nutrients but also reserves a small provision for additional nutrients to sustain the body during lean periods. A diet that strikes the right balance should ideally consist of around 55–60% of total calories from carbohydrates, 10–15% from fats, and 25–35% from proteins. Furthermore, it should also include bioactive phytochemicals such as dietary fiber, antioxidants, and nutraceuticals that offer positive health advantages.

2. Health Benefits of a Balanced Diet

Maintaining a balanced diet comes with a myriad of health benefits, such as:

a) **Increased energy levels:** Consuming a nutritious diet enhances the way the body functions, leading to improved energy levels and a sense of vitality.

b) **Strengthened immune system:** A well-balanced diet supplies the body with the necessary nutrients to bolster the immune system, thus reducing the risk of falling ill.

c) **Weight management:** A balanced diet helps prevent weight gain and can contribute to weight loss when combined with regular exercise, making it an essential component of maintaining a healthy weight.

d) **Prevention and treatment of diseases:** Eating healthily can reduce the risk of developing certain diseases, such as diabetes, cancer, and heart disease. It can also assist in managing existing conditions, like diabetes and high blood pressure.

e) **Stress management:** A balanced diet supports the production of hormones responsible for happiness and promoting a positive mood.

f) General Guidelines for Healthy Eating

To maintain a balanced and healthy diet, consider the following tips:

i) **Embrace raw foods:** Include salads, fruits, and vegetables in your diet to experience the pleasure of eating healthy food without focusing solely on calorie counts.

ii) **Eat mindfully.** Listen to your body's signals, and stop eating when you feel full. This helps you manage your weight and keeps you alert and feeling your best.

iii) **Variety of Foods:** Incorporate a diverse range of foods in your diet, as no single food can provide all the necessary nutrients.

iv) **Snack smartly:** Keep healthy snacks readily available to avoid indulging in unhealthy choices when hunger strikes.

v) **Reduce fat and stimulants:** Limit your intake of saturated fat, caffeine, alcohol, and refined sugar.

vi) **Enjoy what you eat:** Choose foods that you genuinely enjoy, as this encourages a sustainable and enjoyable approach to healthy eating.

3. Hydration and its Role in Vitality

Staying hydrated is one of the best things you can do for your overall health. The human body comprises around 60% water. It's commonly recommended that you drink eight glasses of water per day. Staying hydrated can help support physical performance; prevent headaches and constipation, and more. Drinking enough water each day is also crucial for regulating body temperature, keeping joints lubricated, preventing infections, delivering nutrients to cells, and keeping the organs functioning properly. Besides, it helps in improving sleep quality, cognition, and mood. Here are the 10 evidence-based health benefits of drinking plenty of water:

a. Improved Brain Efficiency
b. Digestive Harmony
c. More Energy
d. Weight loss and management
e. Decreased joint pain
f. Better temperature regulation
g. Kidney stone prevention
h. Healthier Heart
i. Better Detoxification
j. Fewer Headaches

4. Food Groups in Your Diet:

A well-rounded diet should include foods from the following five main groups:

a) **Fruit and Vegetables:** Aim to consume at least 5 portions of a variety of fruits and vegetables every day to receive essential vitamins, minerals, and fiber.

b) **Starchy foods:** Make starchy foods like wholegrain or whole meal varieties a third of your diet to provide energy and essential nutrients.

c) **Milk and dairy foods:** Opt for lower-fat and lower-sugar options for a good source of protein and calcium.

d) **Beans, pulses, fish, eggs, meat, and other proteins:** These foods are rich in protein, vitamins, and minerals necessary for body growth and repair.

e) **Limit saturated fat, sugar, and salt:** Reduce the consumption of saturated fats, sugar, and salt to maintain heart health and overall well-being. Source: Dietary Guidelines for Americans

5. Mediterranean Diet:

As per the article titled "What goes into a Mediterranean diet and how to get started" by Michael Merschel, published on August 23, 2022, by the American Heart Association News, the Mediterranean diet, based on traditional consumption patterns in countries like Greece, Italy, and Spain, has been consistently ranked as the healthiest way to eat. The Mediterranean diet includes a generous amount of fruits and vegetables, healthy fats like olive oil and nuts, lean protein such as seafood, fish, and beans, and complex carbohydrates like whole grains. This dietary pattern has shown significant benefits, with individuals following it experiencing a lower risk of heart attack and stroke. The presence of healthy unsaturated fats in foods like olive oil, nuts, and fish contributes to these protective effects. Research suggests that the Mediterranean diet offers additional advantages beyond cardiovascular health. These potential benefits encompass a reduced risk of diabetes, decreased inflammation, and improved cognitive function.[19]

The DASH diet, promoted by the American Heart Association, is another dietary pattern that focuses on health. It emphasizes vegetables, fruit, legumes, whole grains, low-fat dairy products, nuts, and skinless fish and poultry. Simultaneously, it encourages the reduction of salt, saturated fat, red meat, alcohol, and added sugars, as advocated by the American Heart Association. Incorporating the principles of the Mediterranean diet or similar healthy eating patterns can have a profound impact on overall well-being and longevity. The combination of whole foods, a plant emphasis, and balanced protein and fat intake aligns to live a vibrant and fulfilling life. By nourishing our bodies with the right nutrients and maintaining an active lifestyle, we can thrive in both the physical and mental aspects of life.

6. Never Skip Breakfast:

One of the most crucial rules of healthy eating is to never skip a meal. Skipping meals can have adverse effects on our bodies and overall health. A balanced and nourishing diet involves having three major meals and two snacks between meals. Let us see why, among all the meals, breakfast holds a special significance and should never be skipped.

---

[19]American Heart Association News, published on August 23, 2022.

a) **Breakfast: The Most Vital Meal:** Breakfast is often referred to as the most important meal of the day for a good reason. After a night of restful sleep, our body needs to refuel and replenish its energy reserves. A healthy and wholesome breakfast provides the necessary nutrients and glucose to kick-start our day and maintain stable blood sugar levels. It reduces the likelihood of unhealthy snacking later in the day and helps us feel satisfied.

b) **Mental and Physical Health Benefits:** Eating breakfast regularly has numerous benefits for both physical and mental well-being. It has been observed that individuals who consume breakfast daily tend to have better concentration, problem-solving skills, and eye-hand coordination. They are more alert and creative and they have improved cognitive functions. Moreover, regular breakfast eaters are more likely to maintain a healthy weight and have better body mass index, strength, and endurance. It is also beneficial for a healthy heart.

c) **Consequences of Skipping Breakfast:** When we skip breakfast, we miss out on essential nutrients like vitamins, minerals, and fiber that are vital for a balanced diet. Studies have shown that people who skip breakfast are more prone to obesity. Additionally, skipping breakfast can lead to lower blood sugar levels, slower metabolism, higher hormonal stress levels, reduced stamina, and menstrual irregularities in females.

d) **Avoid Unhealthy Breakfast Choices:** While it is essential not to skip breakfast, it is equally important to make healthy choices. Avoid breakfast options loaded with added sugar or excessive oil. Opt for nutrient-dense foods that provide sustained energy throughout the day.

In conclusion, breakfast plays a pivotal role in our overall health and well-being. It sets the tone for the day and provides us with the necessary nutrients and energy to face the challenges ahead. To ensure a healthy and balanced lifestyle, never skip any meals, especially breakfast. Prioritize nourishing your body with wholesome foods to achieve optimal health and vitality.

Section 3: Weight Management

1. The Importance of Body Mass Index (BMI) and Diet

Maintaining a healthy weight is essential for overall well-being and longevity. According to the American Heart Association, the average daily caloric intake required for metabolic functions is around 2000 calories, though this can vary based on factors like age, gender, and physical activity level.[20]

Weight management involves achieving and maintaining an appropriate body weight through a combination of a balanced diet, regular physical activity, and lifestyle choices. **Body mass index (BMI)** is a critical tool for assessing weight and understanding its relationship to health.

Understanding Body Mass Index (BMI): BMI is calculated using the formula:

BMI = (weight in kilograms) / (height in meters)^2.

Online BMI calculators are readily available for convenience.

As noted in the **Centers for Control and Prevention of Diseases'** report titled "Defining Adult Overweight and Obesity," BMI is a valuable screening tool used by healthcare professionals to identify potential weight-related health risks. The BMI categories are as follows:

---

[20]American Heart Association

1. **Underweight**: BMI less than 18.5

2. **Normal weight**: BMI 18.5 to 24.9

3. **Overweight**: BMI 25 to 29.9

4. **Obesity (Class I, II, and III)**: BMI 30 and above[21]

Importance of Body Mass Index (BMI): Maintaining a healthy BMI is crucial for reducing the risk of various health issues, such as heart disease, type 2 diabetes, hypertension, joint problems, and certain cancers. According to the **Division of Nutrition, Physical Activity, and Obesity** at the National Center for Chronic Disease Prevention and Health Promotion, obesity can lead to type 2 diabetes, heart diseases, and some cancers.[22]

A healthy BMI indicates that an individual's weight is proportional to their height, reducing strain on the body and organs. It also improves overall mobility, energy levels, and quality of life.

2. Type of Diet for Weight Management:

A balanced and nutritious diet is the cornerstone of effective weight management. Here are some dietary guidelines:

a) **Portion Control:** Be mindful of portion sizes to avoid overeating. Focus on consuming smaller, more frequent meals throughout the day rather than large, infrequent ones.

b) **Balanced Nutrients:** Include a variety of foods from all food groups, such as fruits, vegetables, whole grains, lean

---

[21]Centers for Control and Prevention of Diseases, Last reviewed: June 3, 2022
[22]Division of Nutrition, Physical Activity, and Obesity, National Center for Chronic Disease Prevention and Health Promotion, Last reviewed: February 24, 2023.

proteins, and healthy fats. Each nutrient plays a crucial role in supporting the body's functions.

c) **Reduce Added Sugars and Processed Foods:** Limit the intake of sugary beverages, snacks, and processed foods, as they often contain empty calories and offer little nutritional value.

d) **Stay Hydrated:** Drink plenty of water throughout the day. Sometimes, thirst can be mistaken for hunger, leading to unnecessary snacking.

e) **Avoid Crash Diets:** Extreme and restrictive diets that promise rapid weight loss should be avoided. They may lead to nutrient deficiencies and are not sustainable in the long run.

f) **Mindful Eating:** Pay attention to hunger and fullness cues. Eat slowly, savoring each bite, and stop eating when you feel satisfied.

g) **Seek Professional Guidance:** For personalized advice and support, consult a registered dietitian or healthcare professional who can create a tailored diet plan based on individual needs and goals.

Weight management is not just about achieving a specific number on the scale; it is about overall health and well-being. A combination of a balanced diet, regular physical activity, and a healthy lifestyle is the key to maintaining a healthy weight and enjoying a fulfilling life. By being mindful of our BMI and adopting a nutritious diet, we can make positive strides towards achieving and maintaining a healthy weight and better overall health.

Personal Experiences: Embracing a healthy and nourishing diet looks difficult only in the beginning. There are plenty of options out of which we can easily make smart choices about foods that are healthy and delicious too. I don't have the temptation for sugary beverages, snacks, saturated fats, and processed foods, which I stopped taking 20 years ago. We need, on average, around 2000 calories for metabolic functions, depending on our body weight. Adding another around 400 calories that I burn through workouts, I can take daily around 2400 calories, which come from leafy green vegetables, fruits, nuts, curd, cottage cheese, pulses, eggs, and whole grains. I eat chocolate in small amounts once a day.

I have customized my meals to include healthy but tasty foods to my liking. You may find out from the health charts the calories needed daily for metabolic functions for your body weight as well as the calories burned by you in the physical activity and calculate the total calories you can take daily for maintaining your body weight. You may also customize meals of your choice from a variety of vegetables, fruits, whole grains, nuts, milk products, beans, pulses, fish, eggs, lean meat, etc., and other proteins that your taste buds relish. It is advisable to neither eat too much nor too little.

I assure you that by making exercise and healthy eating a habit, you will feel a new rejuvenation in your life.

Section 4: The Importance of Stretching for a Healthy Body and Mind

Stretching is an essential component of any fitness routine. It involves lengthening and elongating muscles to improve their elasticity and relieve tension. Stretching is a simple yet powerful practice that offers a myriad of benefits for your body and mind. Whether you're looking to enhance athletic performance, improve flexibility, or reduce stress, regular stretching can be a valuable addition to your overall health and fitness routine. So take a few moments each day to stretch, breathe, and embrace the many positive effects stretching can bring to your life.

Section 5: Step into Wellness: The Power of Walking

Walking is a simple and accessible form of exercise that offers numerous health advantages. It is suitable for people of all ages and fitness levels, making it an excellent option for incorporating physical activity into daily life. The former President of the USA, Thomas Jefferson, once rightly said, "Walking is the best possible exercise. Habituate yourself to walk very far." Here are some of the key benefits of walking:

a) **Improved Cardiovascular Health:** Walking is a cardiovascular exercise that helps strengthen the heart and improve circulation. It can lower the risk of heart disease, high blood pressure, and stroke.

b) **Weight Management:** Walking can aid in weight management and weight loss by burning calories and boosting metabolism. It is a low-impact exercise that can be sustained for longer durations, making it effective for burning fat.

c) **Joint Health:** Unlike high-impact exercises, walking is gentle on the joints, making it a suitable option for individuals with joint pain or arthritis. It helps improve joint flexibility and reduces the risk of developing joint-related issues.

d) **Boosted Mood and Mental Health:** Walking releases endorphins, which are natural mood boosters. It can reduce stress, anxiety, and depression, promoting overall mental well-being.

e) **Increased Energy Levels:** Regular walking can increase energy levels and reduce feelings of fatigue. It can be a great way to overcome lethargy and boost vitality.

f) **Enhanced Bone Health:** Weight-bearing exercises like walking can help strengthen bones and reduce the risk of osteoporosis.

g) **Better Sleep:** Walking can improve sleep quality and help us fall asleep faster, leading to better overall rest.

h) **Improved Digestion:** Walking after meals can aid digestion and promote a healthier digestive system.

i) **Social Interaction:** Walking with friends, family, or in groups can provide an opportunity for social interaction, which is essential for mental well-being.

j) **Accessible and Cost-Effective:** Walking requires no special equipment or gym membership, making it a cost-effective and convenient form of exercise.

k) **Lowers Risk of Chronic Diseases:** Regular walking has been associated with a reduced risk of chronic diseases, including type-2 diabetes, certain cancers, and metabolic syndrome.

l) **Longevity:** Studies have shown that regular physical activity, including walking, is linked to increased longevity and a lower risk of premature death.

To reap the benefits of walking, it is recommended to aim for at least 150 minutes of moderate-intensity walking per week or 75 minutes of vigorous-intensity walking. This can be achieved through brisk walking or by breaking the duration into shorter, more manageable sessions throughout the day.

Walking is not only an excellent exercise but also a simple way to enjoy nature, explore new surroundings, and add joy to your daily routine. Whether it's a leisurely stroll or a brisk power walk, incorporating walking into your lifestyle can significantly contribute to your overall health and well-being.

Section 6: Healthy Aging and Disease Prevention:

Learn about the factors that contribute to healthy aging, such as maintaining a healthy weight, managing stress, getting quality sleep, and engaging in regular physical activity. The following tips may be useful for healthy aging:

a) **Promoting Longevity**: As per the WHO Report published on October 5, 2023, physical activity reduces symptoms of depression and anxiety, enhances thinking, learning, and judgment skills, and improves overall well-being. Doing a small amount of exercise will keep your body strong and fit as you age. Develop an exercise routine while you are young and then maintain it over the decades to come. This will make you healthier now by managing your weight, building muscles, and reducing stress. It will also benefit your future health by strengthening your bones, improving your balance, and boosting your immune system. An ideal exercise program includes 15–30 minutes of aerobic exercise five times per week and strength training twice per week.

b) **Disease Prevention and Management**: Understand the importance of preventive measures, such as regular health check-ups, screenings, and vaccinations, to identify and address potential health risks.

c) **Managing Chronic Conditions**: Explore strategies for effectively managing chronic conditions, including diabetes, heart disease, arthritis, and respiratory disorders, to maintain a high quality of life.

d) **Prioritizing Sleep and Rest**: Recognize the significance of rest and quality sleep in rejuvenating the body and mind, promoting optimal cognitive function, and supporting overall well-being.

e) **Establishing Healthy Sleep Habits**: Discover practical tips for improving sleep hygiene, creating a relaxing bedtime routine, and cultivating an environment conducive to restful sleep.

f) **Harnessing the Mind-Body Connection:** Understand the profound interplay between the mind and body and how nurturing your mental well-being can positively impact your physical health.

g) **Stress Management:** Explore effective stress reduction techniques, such as meditation, deep breathing exercises, and engaging in activities that bring joy and relaxation.

h) **The Role of Emotional Health:** Learn how emotional well-being influences physical health and discover strategies for fostering positive emotions, cultivating resilience, and nurturing healthy relationships.

By embracing a holistic approach to healthy aging, individuals can promote vitality, well-being, and a high quality of life throughout their later years. It's never too late to adopt healthy habits that contribute to graceful aging and a fulfilling life.

Conclusion: In this chapter, we have explored the foundational elements of nurturing physical vitality to pave the way for lasting bliss. Nurturing your body through regular exercise, nutrition, restorative sleep, and holistic well-being practices forms the foundation for lasting bliss. By prioritizing your physical health, you are sowing the seeds of a radiant, joyful, and purposeful life. As you embark on this journey of physical wellness, remember that small, consistent steps can yield profound transformations.

CHAPTER-7

The Journey Within: Nurturing Mental Health for Lasting Happiness

In the fast-paced and demanding world we live in, mental health has emerged as a critical aspect of overall well-being. Our mental state influences every facet of our lives, shaping our thoughts, emotions, and actions. Just as we invest time and effort in caring for our physical health, it is equally important to prioritize the well-being of our mind. In accordance with the World Health Organization's (WHO) constitution, health is defined as "a state of complete physical, mental, and social well-being and not merely the absence of disease or infirmity" (WHO Constitution).

In this journey within, we will explore the significance of mental health and delve into the practices and insights that can lead us to lasting happiness.

In Chapters 3 and 4, we discussed how spiritual wisdom helps us practice mindfulness and understand the power of our thoughts, enabling us to cultivate gratitude and emotional intelligence, stay optimistic, nurture healthy relationships, and live authentically. Behind the scenes of our emotions and mental states, hormones, the chemical messengers produced by various glands in the body, play a significant role in regulating emotions, stress responses, and overall mental health. In this chapter, we will discuss how the symbiotic relationship between spiritual wisdom and hormonal regulation underscores their combined impact on mental well-being.

Section: 1

1. Understanding Mental Health

At the core of a fulfilling life lies the foundation of a healthy mind. Mental health encompasses not only the absence of mental illness but also the presence of positive traits and emotional resilience. It is a dynamic state that fluctuates in response to life's challenges and joys. Understanding and nurturing our mental health is crucial for fostering a sense of balance, inner peace, and contentment. Embracing spiritual wisdom can lead to remarkable transformations in our mental well-being, bringing harmony and tranquility into our lives. This profound understanding of the mind's power extends beyond mere psychological benefits, as it also intricately intertwines with the complex interactions of hormones within our bodies.

In the pursuit of mental well-being, understanding the interplay between spiritual wisdom and the role of hormones can be enlightening. Let us explore how spiritual wisdom empowers individuals to harness the power of their thoughts, while different hormones play a vital role in shaping emotions and overall mental health.

2. Influence of Spiritual Wisdom on Our Thoughts:

- **Recognizing the Power of Thoughts:** In Chapter 3, we discussed comprehensively the impact of spiritual wisdom on our thoughts. At the core of spiritual wisdom lies the recognition that our thoughts wield immense power in shaping our reality. Positive and optimistic thoughts can imbue us with a sense of harmony, fostering an uplifting atmosphere within our minds and hearts. On the other hand, negative and self-defeating thoughts can plunge us into inner turmoil, leading to anxiety and distress.

- **Mindful Observation and Redirecting Thoughts:** In Chapters 3 and 4, we learned how spiritual wisdom guides us to become more mindful of our thought patterns. By learning to observe our thoughts non-judgmentally, we cultivate self-awareness and gain insights into the root causes of negativity. Through various spiritual practices, such as meditation and introspection, we can develop the ability to redirect our thoughts towards positivity and purpose. This transformational process allows us to take charge of our mental landscape and foster a more resilient mindset. You may refer to Chapter 4 for more details on meditation and introspection.

- **Practicing Mindfulness:** Mindfulness invites us to be fully present in the here and now. By cultivating this awareness, we can break free from the grip of rumination and worries about the past or future, finding solace in the present moment. Mindfulness is a transformative practice that brings profound happiness and well-being into our lives. By embracing the present moment with awareness and acceptance, we cultivate emotional well-being, reduce stress, and foster fulfilling relationships. Mindfulness nurtures gratitude, compassion, and resilience, allowing us to navigate life's challenges with grace and joy. Mindfulness invites us to find joy and fulfillment in the ordinary moments of life. Engaging in everyday activities with full presence and curiosity enhances our appreciation for life's simple pleasures. As we integrate mindfulness into our daily lives, we embark on a journey of self-discovery and inner peace, experiencing the true essence of happiness in each moment.

Section: 2

1. Embracing Emotional Intelligence:

Emotional intelligence empowers us to understand and manage our emotions effectively. By developing empathy and compassion for ourselves and others, we foster healthier relationships and build emotional resilience to navigate life's challenges with grace.

Emotional intelligence, often referred to as EQ, is a vital aspect of our overall well-being that profoundly influences our ability to experience lasting happiness. It involves recognizing, understanding, and effectively managing our emotions and the emotions of others. Studies have confirmed that positive emotions and agreeableness contribute to the development of congenial relationships with others, thereby fostering an increase in social support.[23]

a) **Emotional Intelligence and Self-Awareness:** At the core of emotional intelligence lies self-awareness—the ability to recognize and understand our own emotions. By developing a deep awareness of our feelings, we can identify triggers, strengths, and areas for improvement. Self-awareness allows us to navigate our emotions with grace, enabling us to respond rather than react impulsively to challenging situations. This enhanced self-understanding is a crucial foundation for lasting happiness.

b) **Emotional Regulation and Happiness:** Let us explore the strong correlation between emotional intelligence and happiness and understand how developing EQ can lead to

---

[23]Caspi A, Roberts BW, Shiner RL. Personality development: stability and change. Annu Rev Psychol 2005; 56:453–84.

greater emotional resilience, fulfilling relationships and a more contented and joyful life.

- **Inner Peace and Contentment**: Emotional intelligence empowers us to regulate our emotions effectively. Instead of being overwhelmed by negative emotions, individuals with high EQ develop healthy coping mechanisms, such as mindfulness and self-compassion, which contribute to emotional resilience. By learning to manage emotional highs and lows, we create a stable emotional foundation, fostering inner peace and contentment.

- **Fulfilling Relationships**: Empathy, the ability to understand and share the feelings of others, is an essential component of emotional intelligence. By empathizing with those around us, we form stronger and more meaningful connections, leading to fulfilling relationships.

- **Supportive Social Environment**: People with high EQ are adept at building positive connections and fostering a sense of camaraderie, resulting in a more enjoyable and supportive social environment.

- **Resilience**: Emotional intelligence cultivates a positive outlook on life. Those with high emotional intelligence approach challenges with a growth mindset, seeing them as opportunities for learning and personal growth. This optimistic perspective enhances resilience, enabling individuals to bounce back from adversity and maintain a sense of happiness and hopefulness.

c) **Cultivating Emotional Intelligence:**

- **Self-Reflection:** Regular self-reflection is essential for developing emotional intelligence. Take time to examine your emotions, thought patterns, and reactions to various situations. Meditation or journaling can be helpful tools for gaining deeper insights into your emotional landscape.

- **Active Listening:** Practice active listening when interacting with others. Seek to understand their emotions and perspectives genuinely. This fosters empathy and strengthens your emotional connection with them.

In conclusion, emotional intelligence is a key determinant of lasting happiness. By developing self-awareness, regulating our emotions, and cultivating empathy and social skills, we can create a more fulfilling and contented life. Emotional intelligence enhances our ability to navigate challenges, form meaningful connections, and foster a positive outlook on life. Embrace the journey of emotional intelligence and watch how it enriches your well-being, bringing profound happiness and fulfillment to every aspect of your life.

Section: 3

1. Living Authentically: The Path to Lasting Happiness

Living authentically means being true to oneself and embracing one's values, beliefs, and emotions without pretense or conformity to societal expectations. This authentic way of living is deeply connected to genuine happiness and contentment. Living authentically is a transformative path that leads to lasting happiness and contentment. By embracing self-awareness, aligning with values, and letting go of external expectations, we liberate ourselves from the burden of conformity and external validation. Authentic living fosters genuine connections, inner peace, and personal growth, enhancing our overall well-being. Embracing authenticity empowers us to live with purpose and find genuine happiness in each moment, making it a powerful and transformative way of living.

2. Making Life Meaningful:

Engaging in activities that align with our passions and values creates a sense of fulfillment and gives meaning to our existence. Finding meaning in life is a fundamental human quest that profoundly impacts our overall happiness and well-being. When we lead a life of purpose and significance, we experience a deeper sense of fulfillment and contentment. The secret of the long life of Japanese centenarians is **Ikigai**, the living with a purpose. Let us see the relationship between meaningful living and happiness:

- Meaningful living starts with self-discovery. By understanding our core values, passions, and unique strengths, we gain clarity about what truly matters to us. Embracing our authentic selves allows us to set meaningful goals aligned with our deepest desires, fostering a sense of purpose. Living meaningfully involves aligning our actions with our values and beliefs. When our daily choices reflect our core principles, we experience a profound sense of integrity, which positively impacts our overall well-being.

- A meaningful life often involves contributing to something greater than ourselves. Engaging in acts of kindness, volunteering, or supporting a cause we believe in not only benefits others but also brings a sense of purpose and satisfaction to our own lives.

- Meaningful living involves embracing challenges and viewing them as opportunities for growth. Meaningful relationships with others are the cornerstone of a meaningful life.

- Meaningful living encourages us to prioritize our well-being and personal fulfillment. Taking care of our physical, mental, and emotional health allows us to be the best version of ourselves, contributing to our happiness.

- Meaningful living often entails experiencing moments of transcendence—those awe-inspiring and humbling experiences that connect us to something larger than ourselves. Whether through nature, art, or spiritual practices, these moments enhance our sense of purpose and happiness.

3. Practicing Gratitude for Fulfillment:

Cultivating gratitude is a transformative journey that leads to lasting happiness and contentment. By shifting our perspective and focusing on the positive aspects of life, we can experience a profound sense of well-being. Gratitude reminds us to savor the beauty of life's simple moments, cherish our connections, and find strength in adversity. It goes beyond mere thankfulness for the good things in life; it is an attitude of appreciation and recognition for both the joys and challenges we encounter. When we consciously practice gratitude, we shift our focus from what is lacking to what we already have. It enables us to acknowledge the simple pleasures, meaningful connections, and everyday blessings that often go unnoticed. By embracing gratitude, we open ourselves up to a richer and more meaningful existence.

When faced with adversity, a grateful mindset helps us find silver linings and valuable lessons within the experience. Instead of dwelling on hardships, we learn to appreciate the growth and resilience we gain from overcoming obstacles. This shift in perspective empowers us to approach life with a sense of hope and optimism. Numerous studies have shown that practicing gratitude regularly can significantly enhance our overall happiness and well-being. Grateful individuals tend to experience more positive emotions, reduced stress levels, and improved mental health. By focusing on the blessings in our lives, we become less entangled in negative thought patterns and are better equipped to navigate life's ups and downs with grace.

Incorporating gratitude into your daily life can be a transformative journey, and it can help you along the way. Here are a few tips for developing gratitude.

Tips for cultivating gratitude:

- **Appreciate Yourself:** Gratitude starts with noticing the goodness in life. Recognizing one's own worth and acknowledging personal achievements and virtues can boost self-esteem and create a positive mindset. By appreciating yourself for your past achievements or your present efforts, your talents, and your virtues, you create self-esteem while also expressing gratitude to God.

- **Find a Gratitude Buddy:** Sharing thoughts of gratitude with someone is a great way to sustain motivation that strengthens your emotional skills. Gratitude Visits: Exchange some good memories and offer your support to someone whom you love and can depend upon.

- Gratitude Journaling: By penning down all the little and big things in life that you are thankful for, you cultivate gratitude.

4. Staying Optimistic:

A positive outlook can help us navigate challenges with resilience and hope, promoting mental well-being. Optimism, the ability to maintain a positive outlook even in challenging times, is a powerful tool that influences our happiness and well-being. When we cultivate an optimistic mindset, we can navigate life's obstacles with resilience and hope, ultimately leading to a more fulfilling and joyful existence.

Winston Churchill once said, "A pessimist sees the difficulty in every opportunity; an optimist sees the opportunity in every difficulty."

Optimism acts as a shield against adversity, providing us with the strength to bounce back from setbacks and face challenges head-on.

a) **Shifting Perspectives**: Staying optimistic involves consciously choosing to reframe negative thoughts and situations positively. By shifting our perspectives, we can find hidden opportunities for growth and learning, transforming obstacles into stepping stones towards personal development. Recent research proves that the negative effects of stress and their expected outcomes can be diminished and/or reversed by actively engaging in optimism.

b) **Benefits of Staying Optimistic**:

- Optimism instills hope and positive expectations for the future. Believing in our ability to achieve our goals and envisioning a brighter tomorrow boosts our motivation and propels us towards success, happiness, and a sense of purpose.

- Optimism helps reduce stress, anxiety, and depression, promoting a sense of calm and contentment in our daily lives.

- A hopeful and positive demeanor attracts like-minded individuals, fosters meaningful connections, and nurtures supportive relationships.

- Optimism goes hand-in-hand with gratitude and mindfulness. By appreciating the present moment and counting our blessings, we cultivate a sense of contentment and appreciation for life's small joys.

- In times of uncertainty, staying optimistic helps us manage fear and apprehension. It enables us to focus on solutions rather than dwelling on problems, leading to proactive and constructive decision-making.

- Optimism is contagious and has the power to inspire those around us. By radiating positivity, we can uplift others, create a harmonious environment, and collectively contribute to a happier community.

c) **Staying Optimistic for Mental and Physical Health:**

Having an optimistic outlook goes beyond just feeling good; it can significantly influence various aspects of your life. Optimistic individuals tend to be more committed to their goals, experience greater success, and report higher life satisfaction. Research indicates that optimism can lead to improved mental and physical health.[24]

Here are 10 reasons why strengthening your optimism is a good idea:

- **Optimists Feel Healthier**: Optimistic individuals often perceive themselves as healthier and happier.

- **Optimists Are Healthier**: Studies show that optimism is linked to improved heart health and better cholesterol levels.

- **Optimists Are More Likely to Be Centenarians**: Expecting a long life can actually increase your chances of living longer.

- **Optimists Take Fewer Sick Days**: Optimism may boost your immune system and help you stay healthier.

- **Optimists Are Less Prone to Stress**: Optimistic individuals produce less cortisol, the stress hormone, and experience less perceived stress.

- **Optimists Have Happier Relationships**: Optimistic individuals and their partners tend to have happier romantic relationships.

- **Optimists Have Happier Careers**: Optimists often find their jobs more satisfying and have fewer work-related complaints.

- **Optimists Get More Job Offers and Promotions**: Positive thinking can enhance job hunting and lead to better career prospects.

---

[24]Jessica Cassity, The Benefits of Looking on the Bright Side: 10 Reasons to Think Like an Optimist, Source: Happyify (https://my.happify.com/login/)

- **Optimists Are Better at Bouncing Back**: Optimists tend to cope more effectively with life's challenges and experience less stress and anxiety.

- **Optimists Make Better Athletes**: Optimists use setbacks as motivation to perform better, making them more resilient in sports.

By acting optimistically, even when you don't naturally feel that way, you can reap these benefits. Optimism is not just about seeing the glass as half full; it can improve your overall well-being, relationships, and even your physical health. As we choose to stay optimistic, we unlock the key to happiness, enriching our lives with positivity, hope, and a deep sense of contentment.

5. Fostering a Positive Environment

Nurturing healthy connections with others fosters a support system that can help us navigate life's ups and downs. Relationships provide acceptance, support, and safety, and investing time and energy to create and maintain healthy relationships may be a great source of happiness. Surrounding ourselves with positive influences and a supportive community can significantly impact our mental well-being. Engaging in meaningful connections and nurturing healthy relationships fosters a sense of belonging and support.

6. Getting Enough Sleep:

Prioritizing sufficient and restful sleep is crucial for mental and physical rejuvenation. A **review of research** found evidence that insomnia preceded the development of not only depression but also bipolar disorder and anxiety disorders. The researchers also found a link between insomnia and an increased risk of suicide.[25] The Centers for Disease Control and Prevention (CDC) recommend that people aged 18–60 get 7 or more hours of sleep each night (National Center for Chronic Disease Prevention and Health Promotion, Division of Population Health, last reviewed on September 14, 2022). Restorative sleep for 7-8 hours at night is essential for stress management, improved mood, better performance in physical activities, fewer inflammations, healthier weights, better focus on work, and a lower risk of diabetes and heart disease. According to studies, sleep eases pain and anxiety in the brain. Sleep also helps the brain learn and stay flexible.

- **Tips for Restorative Sleep:** Regular exercise, sleep hygiene, avoiding heavy meals before bedtime, maintaining a regular bedtime, limiting alcohol, and avoiding caffeine in the evening may help get restorative sleep for more than 7 hours at night.

7. Getting Physically Active:

Regular physical activity not only enhances physical health but also boosts mood and mental well-being. You may refer to Chapter 6 for more details on the benefits of physical activity for mental wellness.

8. Coping with stress:

Life often presents us with stressors that can affect our mental health. Learning healthy coping mechanisms, such as exercise, relaxation techniques, meditation, or seeking support from

---

[25]Pigeon W.R., Bishop, T.M., & Krueger, K.M., "Insomnia as a Precipitating Factor in New-Onset Mental Illness: A Systematic Review of Recent Findings," Current Psychiatry Reports, Vol. 19 (44) June 14, 2017. https://doi.org/10.1007/ s11920-017-0802-x

loved ones, equips us to navigate stress and adversity with greater ease. We gleaned from Chapters 3 and 4 how spiritual wisdom plays a great role in managing stress in life. We also learned from Chapter 5 that physical activity is a great way to minimize stress.

9. Seeking Professional Support:

Just as we visit a doctor for physical ailments, seeking professional help for mental health concerns is essential. Trained therapists and counselors provide valuable guidance and tools to overcome challenges and build resilience. As we delve deeper into this exploration of mental well-being, let's transition from understanding the influence of spiritual wisdom to unraveling the intricate dance between our thoughts and the hormones that shape our emotional landscape.

Section: 4

1. The Impact of Hormones on Mental Well-Being:

The Hormonal Orchestra: Behind the scenes of our emotions and mental states, a complex hormonal orchestra orchestrates the symphony of our well-being. Hormones, chemical messengers produced by various glands in the body, play a significant role in regulating emotions, stress responses, and overall mental health.

a) **Serotonin:** Often referred to as the "feel-good" hormone, serotonin plays a vital role in promoting feelings of happiness and well-being. Spiritual practices like meditation and acts of compassion have been linked to increased serotonin levels, contributing to a more balanced emotional state and reducing anxiety. Research has shown that serotonin plays a vital role in mood regulation and various bodily functions, including sleep, appetite, anxiety, digestion, blood clotting, and sexual desire.[26]

b) **Dopamine:** Known as the "reward" hormone, dopamine is associated with feelings of pleasure and motivation. Dopamine, a neurotransmitter, plays a vital role in the brain's reward system and is associated with the sensation of pleasure. Activities like sex, shopping, and even the aroma of freshly baked cookies can trigger a release of dopamine, often termed a "dopamine rush." Intriguingly, there's evidence suggesting that meditation might also lead to increased dopamine release, possibly due to the altered state of consciousness it induces. Engaging in activities that align with one's spiritual values and sense of purpose can trigger dopamine release, fostering a sense of fulfillment and encouraging a positive outlook on life.[27]

c) **Oxytocin:** The Love and Trust Hormone Oxytocin, often affectionately referred to as the "hugging hormone" or the "love hormone," is a remarkable neurotransmitter and hormone produced in the brain's hypothalamus and released by the pituitary gland. It plays a crucial role in social bonding, emotional connections, and overall well-being. Spiritual communities and meaningful relationships can stimulate oxytocin release, strengthen social bonds, and promote emotional well-being.

Key Functions of Oxytocin:

- **Social Bonding:** Oxytocin is released during physical touch, such as hugging, kissing, or cuddling, and it promotes feelings of trust, closeness, and connection. This is why it's

---

[26]J Psychiatry Neurosci2007 Nov; 32(6): 394–399.

[27]Harvard Medical School (July 20, 2021). Dopamine is the pathway to pleasure. Harvard Women's Health Watch

often associated with the bond between mothers and their infants during breastfeeding and childbirth.

- **Love and Emotional Attachment:** Oxytocin is at the heart of romantic relationships. It enhances feelings of love, attachment, and emotional intimacy between partners. When you feel a deep connection with someone, you can thank oxytocin for playing a role.

- **Stress Reduction:** Oxytocin has stress-reducing properties. It counteracts the effects of the stress hormone cortisol and helps to soothe the body's stress response. This is why social support and physical affection can be incredibly comforting during stressful times.

- **Trust and Empathy:** Oxytocin is thought to enhance feelings of trust and empathy. It encourages prosaic behaviors, such as helping others and showing kindness. This hormone is one of the reasons behind the warm, fuzzy feeling you get when you perform acts of kindness or receive them.

Boosting Oxytocin Naturally:

- **Positive Social Interactions:** Engaging in positive social interactions, such as spending quality time with loved ones, deep conversations, or acts of kindness, can boost oxytocin levels.
- **Physical Touch:** Hugging, kissing, holding hands, and physical affection in general can trigger oxytocin release. Skin-to-skin contact, especially in intimate relationships, is a powerful oxytocin booster.
- **Sharing Meals:** Sharing a meal with friends or family can increase oxytocin. It's not just about the food; it's the social connection and bonding that dining together provides.

- **Emotional Openness:** Being emotionally open and vulnerable with someone you trust can stimulate oxytocin release. Sharing your thoughts and feelings fosters deeper connections.

- **Acts of Kindness:** Both performing acts of kindness and receiving them can raise oxytocin levels. Acts of generosity and compassion have a mutual benefit for both the giver and the receiver.

- **Conclusion:** Oxytocin is a remarkable hormone that plays a central role in our ability to connect, bond, and experience love and trust. Nurturing positive social relationships, practicing empathy and kindness, and enjoying physical touch can all contribute to higher oxytocin levels, enhancing our overall sense of well-being and happiness.[28]

2. **The Harmonious Integration of Spiritual Wisdom and Hormonal Balance Synchronizing Body, Mind, and Soul**:

As we've explored the intricate role of hormones in shaping our mental well-being, it becomes increasingly apparent that our physical and emotional states are deeply interconnected. Now, let's delve into the harmonious integration of spiritual wisdom with these hormonal dynamics, creating a holistic approach to nurturing our mental health.

- The integration of spiritual wisdom and hormonal balance offers a holistic approach to mental well-being. When we nurture our spiritual selves through practices that align with our values, we activate neurochemical processes that enhance emotional resilience, reduce stress, and promote a positive outlook.

---

[28]Matt Kandler, Founder, Happyfeed, Brain Chemicals That Make You Happy, July 30, 2019

- **Stress Reduction**: By managing our thoughts and emotions through spiritual practices, we can mitigate the release of stress-related hormones like cortisol. A balanced hormonal response contributes to improved mood and a greater sense of inner peace.

In conclusion, the symbiotic relationship between spiritual wisdom and hormonal regulation underscores their combined impact on mental well-being. Recognizing the power of thoughts and cultivating spiritual practices enables us to harness the potential for positive change within ourselves. Additionally, understanding the role of hormones helps us appreciate the physiological mechanisms that influence our emotions. By embracing this profound synergy, we embark on a journey towards greater mental and emotional harmony, ultimately enriching our lives with purpose, joy, and serenity. As we embark on this journey of nurturing mental health, we recognize that happiness is not merely a destination but a continuous process of self-discovery and growth. By embracing the power of our thoughts and actions and incorporating positive practices into our lives, we unlock the door to lasting happiness within ourselves.

CHAPTER-8

Embracing Aging Blissfully to 100 Years

Embracing the Journey of Aging:

Aging is a natural progression, a journey marked by unique perspectives and opportunities for personal growth. Blissful aging hinges on embracing the wisdom that accompanies age, an essential facet of the journey. Spiritual resilience developed over the years empowers us to view aging as a repository of wisdom and expansion, enabling us to navigate the passage of time with grace and authenticity. Research underscores that adopting a positive perspective on aging bolsters self-esteem, resilience, and coping mechanisms while reducing the likelihood of cognitive decline, depression and chronic ailments. Challenging prevailing stereotypes about aging enables us to extract beauty and potential from every phase of life, fostering a sense of fulfillment that transcends years.

In Chapter 5: **Living with Purpose: Crafting a Blueprint for Fulfillment**, we identified certain truths about aging. In this chapter, we will try to find specific solutions to the areas that need special attention in the eighties and nineties. Let us move forward to embrace the journey of aging as a truth of life and tread it cheerfully.

1. Cultivating Healthy Habits for Fulfillment:

A core aspect of blissful aging lies in the daily choices we make, steering the trajectory of our physical and mental well-being. The canvas of longevity is painted with the brushstrokes of healthy habits, encompassing nourishing nutrition, regular exercise, rejuvenating sleep, and refraining from detrimental behaviors. As discussed in the previous chapters, these choices act as guardians against age-related ailments and elevate our mood, energy, and cognitive prowess. Engaging in meaningful pursuits like mastering new skills, dedicating time to hobbies, volunteering, or embracing purposeful work bestows upon us mental agility, creativity, and a sense of accomplishment. These pursuits would not only invigorate our minds but also infuse life with purpose, achievement, and contentment. Always keep in mind that following healthy habits is of prime importance for blissful aging.

2. Fostering Social Connections:

The threads of social connection form a rich tapestry that fortifies our experience of blissful aging. Companionship with family, friends, and community members serves as a buffer against solitude, loneliness, and loss. These connections offer solace, camaraderie, and practical support, infusing life with joy, love, and shared growth. Furthermore, these relationships broaden our horizons, exposing us to novel perspectives, sparking curiosity, and enriching our lives with diverse experiences.

3. Prioritizing Physical and Mental Well-Being:

We discussed in Chapters 5 and 6 that blissful aging demands a vigilant approach to nurturing physical and cognitive well-being. Within this realm, certain aspects require special attention to ensure a life of vitality and grace.

a) **Cardiovascular Health:** The heart's rhythm sustains the melody of life, circulating vitality to every corner of our being. As the years unfold, our blood vessels and arteries may undergo changes that challenge the heart's efficiency. Nurturing cardiovascular health entails regular exercise, a balanced diet, abstaining from smoking, stress management and restful sleep. By weaving these practices into our lives, we safeguard the heart's enduring vitality and mitigate the risk of high blood pressure, heart diseases, and strokes.

b) **Skeletal and Muscular Resilience:** The architecture of bones, joints, and muscles provides the scaffolding of our existence, enabling us to move through life with grace. With time, bones may exhibit reduced density and strength, rendering them vulnerable to fractures. Muscles, too, may yield to the passage of time, losing mass and flexibility. Through the alchemy of weight-bearing exercises, ample calcium and vitamin D intake, and commitment to healthy weight management, we bolster skeletal and muscular fortitude.

c) **Nurturing Cognitive Brilliance:** Cognitive prowess defines our journey through knowledge, reasoning, and self-expression. The passage of time may introduce variations to this symphony, but our dedication to cognitive health remains steadfast. By engaging in stimulating activities, nurturing social connections, managing emotions, and seeking professional guidance when needed, we may preserve the brilliance of our cognitive abilities.

4. Resilience in the Face of Challenges:

Blissful aging is not an escape from life's trials but rather an arsenal of strength that empowers us to confront them with equanimity. Drawing from the reservoir of spiritual resilience honed over the years, we navigate challenges with unwavering grace. Each trial becomes an avenue for growth, an invitation to shape our evolution. Through this lens, the canvas of blissful aging emerges as an evolving masterpiece, painted with the hues of authenticity and serenity.

5. A Life of Purpose and Unceasing Growth:

In the tapestry of blissful aging extending to 100 years, the threads of purpose and growth remain steadfastly woven. Purpose serves as a guiding light, illuminating each day with significance and resonance. Engaging in pursuits that ignite passions and align with values infuses life with motivation and fulfillment. Spiritual wisdom calls us to contribute to the world's betterment, reminding us that our actions ripple across time and space. Just as the moon reflects the sun's brilliance, our years radiate the luminance of our ikigai—the reason for waking each morning. Research from around the world has affirmed that early retirement often correlates with reduced life expectancy, while purposeful engagement leads to longer, healthier lives.

In conclusion, as life's chapters unfold, the pursuit of blissful aging beckons as an attainable and inspiring goal. It is not a distant utopia, but a horizon that invites us to chart a course of vitality, purpose, and happiness. Through the prism of positive aging, we uncover the secrets to a life that thrives beyond a century. By embracing aging, nurturing physical and mental well-being, weaving a tapestry of social connections, and embarking on a journey of perpetual growth and purpose, we pave the path to a life resonating with joy and meaning. Blissful aging is not merely a distant possibility; it is a reality that awaits us, inviting us to embrace life's progression and dance to its harmonious rhythm. Let us take inspiration from the people of Okinawa and the outstanding centenarians like Nobel Laureate Goodenough and Dr. Calyampudi Radhakrishan Rao for blissfully aging with a purpose.

CHAPTER-9

Experiences Gained and Realizations Made: Navigating Life's Journey

Introduction: In this chapter, I invite you to journey alongside me as I share personal experiences, reflections, and profound realizations that have shaped my perspective on life. We will explore the challenges that tested my resilience, the invaluable lessons that failure taught me, and the moments of triumph that inspired me. As we delve into this exploration of my life's tapestry, you'll discover how self-reflection, determination, and an unwavering connection with the principles discussed in this book have guided me toward a path of lasting bliss. It's the story of the person who has unflinching faith in God and believes that eternal bliss lies in the coherence of spiritual, physical, mental, and emotional domains. Life is a journey for man—for self-realization, improvement, regulation, and spreading happiness.

Section 1:

The Power of Ambition, Self-Belief, and Commitment

It is easy to choose a path of anonymity and lead an empty life, but striving and leading an impactful life requires a burning desire to realize our dreams. Every one of us is blessed by God with unique mental and physical faculties that we can harness to achieve great goals. We learned in Chapter 4 from the teachings of the Bhagavad Gita that we ought to perform our duties selflessly without a feeling of desire. If you follow this golden teaching of the sacred book, you will realize in yourself a roaring ambition to achieve excellence in your life and a unique power to accomplish that. Taking decisions based on deep core values becomes easier. Commitment to the job becomes a way of life.

Let me narrate, to explain this point, an anecdote of my posting as Superintending Engineer in the year 2005 at Jalandhar, an industrial city and a hub of social and political activities. Just after my posting, on inspection of a 66 KV grid substation, I was stunned to know that the supply to the busiest bazaar and posh areas of the city was being switched off as a part of the load-shedding. After studying the power distribution system of the area, I came to know that the load of the substation can be easily shifted to another substation. And that was done within days, giving a big relief to important areas suffering unnecessarily for a long period of time. The initiative was noticed by the people and highly appreciated. I believe that achieving big goals becomes easy if driven by an ambition to achieve excellence. Thanks to my beliefs in the Bhagavad Gita, I intend to align my thoughts and actions with my deeper core values. Commitment to the job has always been a priority.

A belief that everything can be accomplished if pursued with dedication makes the tasks easier. You ought to have the will and determination to pursue big goals.

The great philosopher and thinker Aristotle rightly said, "Excellence is never an accident. It is always the result of high intention, sincere effort, and intelligent execution; it represents the wise choice of many alternatives; choice not chance, determines your destiny."

I recall that at the time of my first posting in the Punjab State Electricity Board, I was confronted with a few challenging tasks that had been pending for the last six months. A belief in myself and an ambition to excel inspired me to accomplish the tasks efficiently. The effect of that was an improvement in the power supply position in the vast areas of the city and hundreds of villages falling under the jurisdiction of the subdivision, leading to appreciation from the public and the senior officers. During the course of my professional career as well as in leadership roles, I always believed that the key to success is to identify what your duties demand from you, fix ambitious targets accordingly, and put in your best efforts to achieve the targets. Of course, my services were well recognized, and after a commendable service of 34 years, I retired as Engineering-in-Chief in the department.

In the leadership role of the Alumni Association of my Alma Mater, it looked like an impossible task to organize the first ever Global Alumni Meet overseas, but the efforts driven by self-belief and ambition made it possible to organize a very successful, well-attended Alumni Meet in Houston, USA. In order to build bridges across alumni all over the world, it was conceived for the first time to invite the distinguished PEC alumni settled in the USA as chief guests at the three successive alumni meets. As a result, the participation of the alumni in the activities of the Alumni Association and the institute increased significantly.

Of course, there were also a few challenges, one of which was introducing e-voting for the first time in the elections of the Alumni Association. Due to prolonged COVID, the efforts to make it possible came to a halt, and at times it looked like a dead end; however, after the pandemic, the task of e-voting was promptly resumed with spirited efforts. Ultimately, the issue was resolved with patience and persuasion, and the alumni across the world participated in the elections through e-voting for the first time. Certainly, this was another great move towards building bridges across the alumni. The lesson learned is very clear: one should continue to perform actions righteously in discharge of one's duties, as preached by the Bhagavad Gita, without caring for the fruits of the actions.

Of course, the capacity to bounce back against the odds is another essential aspect of happiness. An optimistic outlook makes the tasks easier, enabling the achievement of big targets. Furthermore, accomplishments create self-worth and are a great source of inspiration and fulfillment, one of the major factors contributing to sustained happiness.

Let me share my experience regarding an important aspect of leadership roles. The differences of opinion among the team members are natural. If we disagree on any point under consideration, we should openly, honestly, and respectfully present an opposing opinion instead of simply going along with what's presented, as it improves the quality of the team work. However, before presenting an opposing opinion, we must satisfy ourselves that it would be in the interest of the organization, and we are not opposing for the sake of opposing. In such difficult situations, we may seek guidance from Chapter 2 of the Bhagavad Gita, wherein Lord Krishna urges Arjuna to perform his duty as a warrior without caring for the results. We should identify what our duties demand from us and perform actions righteously in the interest of the organization without any element of fear or criticism. Also, our actions should be selfless, without any desire for praise.

I attribute my success in my professional career and in the leadership roles in the alumni association of my alma mater, Punjab Engineering College, Chandigarh, to my ambition to excel, self-belief, and commitment. I believe that they are great driving forces, enabling the accomplishment of ambitious goals in an elegant manner.

Section 2:

Introspect, Improve, and Excel

Life is a journey for man for self-realization, improvement, regulation, and spreading happiness. By following the teachings of the Bhagavad Gita, we inculcate various virtues such as equanimity, righteousness, truthfulness, courage, fearlessness, compassion, self-regulation, communication skills, and building and sustaining relationships. By learning the art of living with a purpose, we develop self-belief, enabling us to accomplish the toughest tasks. Consider yourself a blessed child of God, and practice gratitude by appreciating what you have and what you have achieved. This will help you cultivate a positive mindset and enhance your self-belief. You don't need to replicate others. Taking care of yourself physically, mentally, and emotionally, getting enough sleep, and exercising regularly cultivate a positive mindset, enhancing your self-belief. One of the best ways to develop self-belief is to act on it. If you do not let fear or doubt stop you from pursuing your dreams, you will realize that you are more capable than you think.

We have personal weaknesses too, but by acknowledging and addressing them, we move forward on the journey to self-improvement.

I recall that I have been very ambitious since childhood. However, despite enough self-belief and a very good academic record, I suffered from anxiety as well as anger and wasted many valuable years before I consciously started to overcome them. Meditation and introspection help us practice mindfulness, enabling us to overcome weaknesses like anger and anxiety.

Section 3:

Navigating Choices and Embracing Opportunities

We gleaned from Chapter 5: Living with a Purpose: Crafting a Blueprint for Fulfillment that the selection of a career is a great life decision that lays the foundation of happiness for the rest of the life. While making a choice of career, you must align it with your aptitude as well as your interest. Let me share my experiences at this point. As mentioned earlier, I excelled in academics in school. However, on the day of admission to the engineering college, I was clueless about the branch to be opted for. I was very ambitious and dreamed simultaneously of many career options, one of which was the Indian Police Service. The pursuit of my dream of joining the Indian Police Service fuelled ambition, leading to plans for post-graduation studies and hostel life. Yet, complacency thwarted my intentions, and I missed the opportunity. However, life had other plans, and I was selected as a sub-divisional officer in the Punjab State Electricity Board, marking the beginning of a successful career. Despite this, the aspiration for the UPSC Exam for Indian Police Service never waned, and I took a leave of absence to prepare diligently. Though narrowly missing, the experience broadened my perspective and enhanced my expression of views. I attribute the missed opportunity to a lack of a single-minded approach. The selection of a career based on aptitude as well as interest is a great driving force. By including that in the blueprint of your life, you eliminate all those confusions that you may otherwise have to face while moving from one stage to the next in your academic career.

Section 4:

Taking Decisions with Intellect

As learned in Chapter 4, the wisdom of the Bhagavad Gita helps us take prompt decisions appropriately. Such decisions based on deep core values generally stand you in good stead. However, when we make decisions based on emotions rather than intellect, they may cause misery. Let me narrate an incident from the early years of my married life to elaborate on this point. We were on a pilgrimage in the hills, at a distance of around 500 kilometers from my native place. The temple was atop a hill, each side 13 kilometers up and down from the base station. After visiting the temple, I asked the car driver to set in for the back journey, despite his advice to me to start the next day in the morning as he was feeling sleepy. Ignoring his advice, I persuaded him to start the journey back home. It was a bad decision based on emotions rather than intellect. Thanks to God, we had a miraculous escape as the driver fell asleep while driving and the car landed in wet paddy fields 15 feet below the road level after passing in between eucalyptus trees at a distance of 2 to 3 feet on either side. The lesson learned was loud and clear: decisions should always be taken with intellect rather than emotions.

Section 5:

Relationships: Bonds That Shape Us

In Chapter 5, you understood the importance of crafting a blueprint of life—the selection of the right career and life partner for your dreams, developing charts for physical activity, and maintaining a balanced, nourishing diet. The selection of a life partner is one of the most difficult decisions, and you must align it with your deeper core values. At the time of my marriage, it was very clear in my mind that my wife should be attractive, a Government College lecturer, and spiritual in outlook. I didn't bow to social pressures and ultimately got the companion of my dreams. The advantage is that we maintain fondness for each other despite minor differences off and on, and there is hardly any difference on major issues such as buying a house or place of settlement, transfers, etc.

The key to harmonious relations is to understand the emotions of each other and learn the art of living happily with differences. Believing that a marital relationship is a spiritual bond enables us to understand each other's emotions and lead an authentic life filled with happiness.

Companionship with family, friends, and community members offers solace, camaraderie, and practical support, infusing life with joy, love, and shared growth. Emotional intelligence is a key determinant of lasting happiness. I have observed that people born with emotional intelligence are more successful in their careers and relationships. Introspection is a great tool for self-improvement. By developing self-awareness, regulating our emotions, and cultivating empathy and social skills, we can create a more fulfilling and contented life.

Section 6:

Nurturing Physical Well-Being:

In Chapter 6, we learned that physical fitness is not a goal that is once achieved and that is done. The nurturing of physical well-being is a journey that starts in the adolescent period and continues throughout the aging process. Undoubtedly, physical wellness is the fountainhead of happiness, and we ought to follow the sound principles of physical activity and a balanced, nutrient-enriched diet in a religious manner to live a healthy, happy, and long life.

The renowned yoga guru and spiritual thinker, B.K.S. Iyengar, has rightly said: Health is a state of complete harmony of the body, mind, and spirit. When one is free from physical disabilities and mental distractions, the gates of the soul open.[29]

When I passed out of the engineering college, I realized that my physical appearance and sensitivity needed attention. Embracing a disciplined exercise routine and a healthy diet, I underwent a remarkable transformation, instilling newfound confidence. For the last three decades, I have been regular with my morning walk and a swimming session in the evening. I have developed taste buds for healthy foods to my liking. Over the years, I have realized that a focus on health, fitness, and meditation is a gate to a fulfilling life. You may follow the teachings of the Bhagavad Gita or your own spiritual beliefs to create a symphony of inner peace and calmness leading to mental wellness. You may consciously practice gratitude, optimism, love, empathy, and kindness, as they go a long way in boosting our mental wellness. Practicing meditation and mindfulness is a great idea for creating inner peace. Regular exercise, a nourishing diet, and a positive attitude towards life, result in healthy biorhythms, sound sleep, a good appetite, and a boost in mood, leading to blissfulness.

---

[29]Light on Life: The Yoga Journey to Wholeness, Inner Peace, and Ultimate Freedom. Book by B.K.S. Iyengar (p. 48), September 19, 2006.

Ongoing Battles Within: Overcoming Desires and Happiness

We gleaned in Chapters 2 and 3 that most of our miseries are due to our unbridled desires. We came to realize that the true measure of happiness is peace with one's self rather than material possessions. We understood that an ongoing struggle exists within us—a constant battle between our innate sensual desires and the noble compass of our spiritual values. These unrestrained urges can be likened to untamed stallions, constantly tugging at the reins of our minds. Yet within this tempest lies a challenge that is both arduous and profoundly transformative. The endeavor to rein in our senses is a pursuit of great worth, a conquest that unveils our inner strength and potential.

In the labyrinth of our existence, there stand three perilous gates—lust, greed, and attachment—leading to the abyss of spiritual decay. However, we may control these vices by conquering our minds, as explained in Chapter 4, by following the teachings of the Bhagavad Gita. Vigilance becomes our armor, shielding us from these perilous paths. In those moments when the conflict between our higher ideals and the pull of earthly desires emerges, let the soft whisper of our soul guide us.

Through mindfulness and introspection, we navigate this inner battlefield. By silencing the cacophony of cravings, we find solace in the realm of our deepest truths. It is here, amidst the chaos and serenity, that we realize the profound power of our choices. Every time we choose the path of self-mastery, we nurture the blossoming of our spiritual essence.

Let us forge ahead, ever vigilant, for this is not a solitary confrontation but a collective human struggle. As we strive to align our inner compass with the North Star of our spiritual values, we become beacons of inspiration, casting a guiding light for ourselves and those who walk beside us on this path of self-discovery.

Conclusion: As our journey through my life's experiences and realizations comes to a close, I extend an invitation for you to embark on your own voyage of introspection. May my stories inspire you to reflect on your own path, guiding you toward the transformative realms of self-improvement, unwavering determination, and a profound connection with spirituality! Through the highs and lows, the joys and sorrows, and the wisdom gained from challenges and triumphs, we uncover the tapestry of life's essence—the pursuit of lasting bliss. Let these insights serve as a testament that within our journey's tapestry, it is in our conscious choices, unyielding self-belief, and commitment to personal growth that we carve a legacy of fulfillment and boundless joy. By embracing a transformative life through self-improvement, determination, and spirituality, we create coherence in our spiritual, physical, mental, and emotional domains, leading to blissfulness. Let us embark upon our journey for 100 years of happiness with a belief in ourselves, determination, and faith in God.

REFERENCES

1. B.K.S. Iyengar, John J. Evans, and Douglas Abrams (2006), "Light on Life: The Yoga Journey to Wholeness, Inner Peace, and Ultimate Freedom," p. 43, Rodale.
2. B.KS. Iyengar, https://www.azquotes.com/quote/849981.
3. Mahatma Gandhi, Jawaharlal Nehru, and Rabindranath Tagore (1968). "Wit and Wisdom of Gandhi, Nehru, and Tagore: Being a Treasury of Over Ten Thousand Invaluable and Inspiring Thoughts, Views, and Observations on About Eight Hundred Subjects of Popular Interest, Collected from the Speeches and Writings of These Three Great Leaders of Modern India."
4. Mahatma Gandhi, Anand T. Hingorani, Ganga Anand Hingorani (1985). The Encyclopedia of Gandhian Thoughts.
5. Ravi Shankar, Ravi Shankar (Sri Sri) (2005), Wisdom for the New Millennium.
6. Tony Robbins Quotes: Fear, Decision, Made.
7. Michael Jordan AZ Quotes: Inspirational, Basketball, Winning
8. John C. Maxwell (2007), "Leadership Principles for Graduates: Create Success in Life One Day at a Time," p. 114, Thomas Nelson Inc.
9. John C. Maxwell Inspirational, Decisions You Make, and Important
10. John C. Maxwell (2011), "The 360-Degree Leader with Workbook: Developing Your Influence from Anywhere in the Organization," p. 85, Thomas Nelson Inc.
11. Oprah Winfrey, Janet Lowe (1998) "Oprah Winfrey speaks: insight from the world's most influential voice," John Wiley and Sons. https://www.azquotes.com/author/15820-Oprah_Winfrey

12. Facebook post by John C. Maxwell from September 25, 2014
13. Tony Robbins (2012), "Awaken the Giant Within," p. 400, Simon and Schuster
14. Kathleen Doheny, "The Healing Power of Friendship Grows with Age", Medically reviewed by Justin Laube (Everyday Health, Reviewed: April 26, 2019)
15. Sport at the New Frontier: The Soft American". Sports Illustrated, Volume 13, Issue 26, pp. 14–17, December 26, 1960.
16. vB Hjelmborg J, Iachine I, Skytthe A, Vaupel JW, McGue M, Koskenvuo M, et al. (April 2006), "Genetic influence on human lifespan and longevity," Human Genetics, 119 (3):312–321.DOI:10.1007/s00439-006-0144-PMID-16463022.S2CID8470835.
17. Moore SC, Patel AV, Matthews CE, Berrington de Gonzalez A, Park Y, Katki HA, et al. (2012) "Leisure time physical activity of moderate to vigorous intensity and mortality: a large pooled cohort analysis". PLOS Medicine 9(11): e1001335.   DOI: 10.1371/journal.pmed.1001335,PMC 3491006.PMID, 23139642.
18. Durstine, J. Larry. "Physical activity, exercise, and chronic diseases: A brief review." Sports Medicine and Health Science (SMHS) Journal, Department of Exercise Science, University of South Carolina, Columbia, SC, USA Published on December 26, 2019
19. American Heart Association News, published on August 23, 2022.
20. American Heart Association
21. Centers for Control and Prevention of Diseases, Last Reviewed: June 3, 2022

22. Division of Nutrition, Physical Activity, and Obesity, National Center for Chronic Disease Prevention and Health Promotion, Last Reviewed: February 24, 2023.
23. Caspi A, Roberts BW, Shiner RL. Personality development: stability and change. Annu Rev Psychol 2005; 56:453–84.
24. Jessica Cassity, The Benefits of Looking on the Bright Side: 10 Reasons to Think Like an Optimist, Happyify (https://my.happify.com/login/)
25. Pigeon, W.R., Bishop, T.M., & Krueger, K.M. "Insomnia as a Precipitating Factor in New-Onset Mental Illness: A Systematic Review of Recent Findings" Current Psychiatry Reports, Vol. 19 (44) June 14, 2017. https://doi.org/10.1007/ s11920-017-0802-x.
26. J Psychiatry Neurosci2007 Nov; 32(6): 394–399.
27. Harvard Medical School (July 20, 2021). Dopamine is the pathway to pleasure. Harvard Women's Health Watch
28. Matt Kandler, Founder, Happyfeed, Brain Chemicals That Make You Happy, July 30, 2019.
29. Light on Life: The Yoga Journey to Wholeness, Inner Peace, and Ultimate Freedom. Book by B.K.S. Iyengar (p. 48), September 19, 2006.

Website Links:

- Bhagavad Gita 2.62:[https://vivekavani.com/b2v62/]

- Bhagavad Gita 2.2: [https://vivekavani.com/b2v2/]

- Bhagavad Gita 2.3: [https://vivekavani.com/b2v3/]

- Bhagavad Gita 2:7: [https://vivekavani.com/b2v7/]

- Bhagavad Gita 2:8: [https://vivekavani.com/b2v8/]

- Bhagavad Gita 2.31: [https://vivekavani.com/b2v31/]

- Bhagavad Gita 2.32: [https://vivekavani.com/b2v32/]

- Bhagavad Gita 2.33: [https://vivekavani.com/b2v33/]

- Bhagavad Gita 2.38: [https://vivekavani.com/b2v38/]

- Bhagavad Gita 2.47: [https://vivekavani.com/b2v47/]

- Bhagavad Gita 2.48: [https://vivekavani.com/b2v48/]

- Bhagavad Gita 2.51: [https://vivekavani.com/b2v51/]

- Bhagavad Gita 2.56: [https://vivekavani.com/b2v56/]

- Bhagavad Gita 2.57: [https://vivekavani.com/b2v57/]

- Bhagavad Gita 3.2: [https://vivekavani.com/b3v2/]

- Bhagavad Gita 3.4: [https://vivekavani.com/b3v4/]

- Bhagavad Gita 3.5: [https://vivekavani.com/b3v5/]

- Bhagavad Gita 3.6: [https://vivekavani.com/b3v6/]

- Bhagavad Gita 3.7: [https://vivekavani.com/b3v7/]

- Bhagavad Gita 3.19: [https://vivekavani.com/b3v19/]

- Bhagavad Gita 3.30: [https://vivekavani.com/b3v30/]

- Bhagavad Gita 3.36: [https://vivekavani.com/b3v36/]

- Bhagavad Gita 3.37: [https://vivekavani.com/b3v37/]

- Bhagavad Gita 3.38: [https://vivekavani.com/b3v38/]

- Bhagavad Gita 3.39: [https://vivekavani.com/b3v39/]

- Bhagavad Gita 3.40: [https://vivekavani.com/b3v40/]

- Bhagavad Gita 3.41: [https://vivekavani.com/b3v41/]

- Bhagavad Gita 3.43: [https://vivekavani.com/b3v43/]

- Bhagavad Gita 5:18: [https://vivekavani.com/b5v18/]

- Bhagavad Gita 5:20: [https://vivekavani.com/b5v20/]

- Bhagavad Gita 5:25: [https://vivekavani.com/b5v25/]

- Bhagavad Gita 6:5: [https://vivekavani.com/b6v5/]

- Bhagavad Gita 6:6: [https://vivekavani.com/b6v6/]

- Bhagavad Gita 6.7: [https://vivekavani.com/b6v7/]

- Bhagavad Gita 6:13: [https://vivekavani.com/b6v13/]

- Bhagavad Gita 6:15: [https://vivekavani.com/b6v15/]

- Bhagavad Gita 6:24: [https://vivekavani.com/b6v24/]

- Bhagavad Gita 6:28: [https://vivekavani.com/b6v28/]

- Bhagavad Gita 6:32: [https://vivekavani.com/b6v32/]

- Bhagavad Gita 6:35: [https://vivekavani.com/b6v35/]

- Bhagavad Gita 6:36: [https://vivekavani.com/b6v36/]

- Bhagavad Gita 9:18: [https://vivekavani.com/b9v18/]

- Bhagavad Gita 9:22: [https://vivekavani.com/b9v22/]

- Bhagavad Gita 9:29: [https://vivekavani.com/b9v29/]

- Bhagavad Gita 10:3: [https://vivekavani.com/b10v3/]

- Bhagavad Gita 10:8: [https://vivekavani.com/b10v8/]

- Bhagavad Gita 10:10: [https://vivekavani.com/b10v10/]

- Bhagavad Gita 10:11: [https://vivekavani.com/b10v11/]

- Bhagavad Gita 10:15: [https://vivekavani.com/b10v15/]

- Bhagavad Gita 10:16: [https://vivekavani.com/b10v16/]

- Bhagavad Gita 10:17: [https://vivekavani.com/b10v17/]

- Bhagavad Gita 10:18: [https://vivekavani.com/b10v18/]
- Bhagavad Gita 10:20: [https://vivekavani.com/b10v20/]
- Bhagavad Gita 12.13: [https://vivekavani.com/b12v13/]
- Bhagavad Gita 13:8: [https://vivekavani.com/b13v8/]
- Bhagavad Gita 13:31: [https://vivekavani.com/b13v31/]
- Bhagavad Gita 14:5: [https://vivekavani.com/b14v5/]
- Bhagavad Gita 14:6: [https://vivekavani.com/b14v6/]
- Bhagavad Gita 14:16: [https://vivekavani.com/b14v16/]
- Bhagavad Gita 16:1: [https://vivekavani.com/b16v1/]
- Bhagavad Gita 16:4: [https://vivekavani.com/b16v4/]
- Bhagavad Gita 16:5: [https://vivekavani.com/b16v5/]
- Bhagavad Gita 16.21: [https://vivekavani.com/b16v21/]
- Bhagavad Gita 16:24: [https://vivekavani.com/b16v24/]
- Bhagavad Gita 17:8: [https://vivekavani.com/b17v8/]
- Bhagavad Gita 17:11: [https://vivekavani.com/b17v11/]
- Bhagavad Gita 17:14: [https://vivekavani.com/b17v14/]
- Bhagavad Gita 17:17: [https://vivekavani.com/b17v17/]
- Bhagavad Gita 17:20: [https://vivekavani.com/b17v20/]
- Bhagavad Gita 17.28: [https://vivekavani.com/b17v28/]